INGLESE da leggere, da ridere, da imparare
10 racconti originali e tanti esercizi e approfondimenti per migliorare divertendosi

Testi: Emanuela (Emy) Siano e David (Dave) Dickens
Editing: Laura Scolari

Redazione Gribaudo
Via Garofoli, 262
37057 San Giovanni Lupatoto (VR)
redazione@gribaudo.it

Responsabile editoriale: Franco Busti
Responsabile di redazione: Laura Rapelli
Responsabile grafico: Meri Salvadori
Fotolito e prestampa: Federico Cavallon, Fabio Compri
Segreteria di redazione: Daniela Albertini

FSC
www.fsc.org
MISTO
Carta
da fonti gestite in
maniera responsabile
FSC® C101934

Stampa e confezione: Grafiche Busti srl, Colognola ai Colli (VR),
azienda certificata FSC®-COC con codice CQ-COC-000104

Socio Unico Giangiacomo Feltrinelli Editore srl
Via Andegari, 6 - 20121 Milano
info@gribaudo.it - www.feltrinellieditore.it/gribaudo/

Prima edizione: 2016 [7(M)] 978-88-580-1490-5

EMANUELA SIANO
DAVID DICKENS

INGLESE
da leggere da ridere da imparare

**10 RACCONTI ORIGINALI
E TANTI ESERCIZI E APPROFONDIMENTI
PER MIGLIORARE DIVERTENDOSI**

GRIBAUDO

HELLO!

Laugh and Learn

Abbiamo corretto gli errori generici di chi sta imparando l'inglese con *Right or Wrong?*, quelli che si fanno al lavoro con *Right or Wrong? At Work*, ora tocca a te! Queste *short stories* servono per farti fare un po' di pratica con il tuo (ormai quasi perfetto?) inglese. Sono dieci storie divertenti, con molto contenuto da ispezionare, spulciare, saggiare. Le storie sono catalogate in due categorie: Ae per l'*American English* e Be per il *British English*, per offrirti la possibilità di comprendere al meglio anche le differenze tra queste due culture che hanno una lingua in comune... in cui non sempre tutto coincide.

Dopo ogni storia troverai esercizi, attività divertenti e spiegazioni chiare e concise che ti aiuteranno a comprendere e applicare nel modo corretto le regole più importanti, ad ampliare il tuo vocabolario e, in generale, ad acquisire un po' della scioltezza tipica dei madrelingua. In fondo al libro troverai qualche pagina da usare per scrivere traduzioni, note, appunti...

- **GOT IT?** La classica *reading comprehension*, dove puoi rispondere ad alcune domande relative al testo per verificarne la comprensione.

- **IN OTHER WORDS** Prova a dire con altre parole un'espressione o una frase.

• **KEY WORDS - Vocabulary** Approfondimento per mettersi alla prova cercando di capire il significato di molte parole.

• **FIND THEM OUT!** Il cruciverba dei *phrasal verbs*, con tanti verbi fraseologici da ripassare/imparare, perché non se ne conoscono mai abbastanza! Oppure GUESS!: invece di trovare i *phrasal verbs*, devi indovinarne il significato!

• **A BIT MORE... - IDIOMS/SLANG & MORE** Un approfondimento davvero utile per apprendere nuovi termini, per padroneggiare espressioni idiomatiche e gergali, per conoscere qualche curiosità.

• **CULTURE SHOCK! American English vs British English** Le principali differenze, tra inglese americano e britannico. Per evitare qualsiasi fraintendimento!

• **FOCUS ON...** Brevi e chiari approfondimenti grammaticali, sulla pronuncia e molto altro.

• **GRAMMAR TOPIC** Per affrontare gli argomenti di grammatica più "scottanti", prendendo spunto dal testo della storia.

• **LOST IN TRANSLATION** Esercizi di traduzione specifici per mettere in pratica subito quello che si è imparato.

• **LOST IN TRANSLATION - MIX IT UP!** Il grande esercizio di traduzione finale, con tutto ciò che è stato trattato nella sezione esercizi... questo sì che sarà un vero *big final test*!

• **I NUMERI NEI CERCHI BLU** si riferiscono ai paragrafi in cui potete trovare le parole e le espressioni presenti negli esercizi e negli approfondimenti.

... and much more! Let's get started!
ENJOY.

Emy
Dave

Stories

AMERICAN ENGLISH

American English

The American Dream

STORY 1

1 I'm Mary and **I've just turned 40**. I was sixteen years old when I first went to the States. You've probably heard this exchange-year story **tons of times** but hey, you haven't heard MY story. The only way you can have such an experience at that age is by being completely "unaware": "not **aware**" of what you are doing! You don't think too much, you don't rationalize anything. How I love that feeling! "Just do it" (which has nothing to do with the famous brand we all know).

2 So there I was, in Monteforte, my parents' native land (less than a thousand people), on a beautiful summer holiday, waiting for a phone call that would change my life forever (now you go "ooooooh"). Oh yes. I was also waiting for the ice-cream van. And it did arrive! The phone call, I mean... well, also the ice-cream, but I was too busy on the phone. They had finally found my American host family.

I had to leave. No more excuses, not that I had one at the time, not like when I even find excuses not to go to the toilet 'cause I'm too **lazy** to get up... I remember that exact moment (the phone call not the toilet) as if it were yesterday and of course now you expect me to say I felt thrilled and excited, but I actually felt almost nothing: completely "unaware".

3 I just had that **dumb** smile (do I still have it?!) on my face and I told my parents I was leaving in two weeks. They seemed more excited than me, I never understood if they were happy for me or happy to be without me. I packed half of my closet and left. Fortunately, back then, the rules at the airport were not so strict, so I was able to take some bottles of water with me (in case they don't sell wa-

ter in the States) and all the medicine my mom gave me (all kinds of things to cure any possible disease).

4 After three days in NYC with the staff and other students from all over the world, **they dropped us off** at the airport and **left us alone**, **facing up to** our new life and destiny. **Can you picture me there?** At JFK airport, all alone, wondering what I was supposed to do. I found my gate and sat there waiting... and waiting... and waiting. It was like waiting for Godot[1], the plane wasn't there! Then God (or Godot, maybe) helped me. An angel **showed up**, a black angel girl, telling me they'd changed the gate. At last! When the plane landed I clapped my hands, too late **to figure out** I was the only one clapping the pilot, so I pretended I was squashing a mosquito.

5 I was in Buffalo, where my host family was still waiting for me (poor them) to go to Lockport, their (small) hometown. I was getting a bit nervous... was I starting to realize where I was?! No, I had to pee. My new family helped me with my bags and we went towards our car (I felt like it was a bit mine already). They started to ask so many questions in such a strange language (English?! Is that the English I study at school?!): cewoijciojcer? Hwohwqiohdw? Cjoiwjwiju? I'm sure I looked like Scrat[2] in *Ice Age* when he's without his nut: lost. So here we are, me and my new American family, talking... trying to talk, trying to have a sort of dialogue! I noticed there was a word they kept repeating, it sounded something like "dou". I was too curious (still am) and I asked "What does 'dou' mean?" Of course it took a while to understand the exact word I meant and in the end it was "though"! The explanation was even harder to understand, so **I gave up**.

6 We arrived home, **safe and sound**. It was all new for me and I had a lot of problems **adjusting**, they call it "culture shock". And it was a real shock to **find out** I had to do my own **laundry**! I have a typical Italian family, a typical Italian mother that does everything for me, but I learnt fast, I had to. I started school and I was shocked again: I had to wake up at 5.30 am to get the bus!

1. *Waiting for Godot* is an absurdist play by Samuel Beckett, in which two characters wait endlessly and in vain for the arrival of someone named Godot. 2. Scrat is one of the main characters in the *Ice Age* movies, a squirrel who is obsessed with collecting acorns, constantly putting his life in danger to obtain and defend them.

7 At school they had amazing classes like Cooking, Photography and Ethics. School was the greatest thing that happened to me there. The first girls I met were very enthusiastic to meet me and they loved the fact I was Italian... really? Ok, wow. They forced me to become a girl scout... me, the one that washes her hands every five minutes, the one who screams if she sees a mosquito. Anyway, it was another new experience in my life, so I accepted. Come on girl, **go for it**! – I said to myself. Once, we went into the woods and it was so cold I couldn't even talk (which was ok since my English was still poor), my feet couldn't move and I was thinking "**I'm not good at this, I can't stand it anymore**". But then my friend smiled at me and said "Let's light a fire and have **marshmallows and chocolate**!". I had no idea what that was, but I understood the word "chocolate" and that was enough **to cheer me up**.

8 The day after we went to school together, we took Latin. Can you believe it? I had to translate things from Latin into English and vice versa. The funny thing about it? We had a great teacher: he wanted to make me feel comfortable so he dyed his hair with the colors of the Italian flag, green white and red... the best teacher ever! My Latin class was great and **we all became very close**. Once, we went to a party together and I had a very good time, except for the music, they played very old songs. There was also a **fun fair** and I played one of those stupid games where you have to shoot with a fake gun, hit some balls hung on a wall to win a prize, but you never win in such games... or I should say you hardly ever win, because I did win! I won a packet of **peanut butter cups**, something you eat and either die or get fat. Well, I got fat, real fat! But I just love **junk food**.

9 A few days after the party I started to feel very tired and something strange appeared on my forehead, like a **pimple** but it wasn't a pimple. I started to think I had something really bad, that I would die there in the States, eating peanut butter and French fries. But I had caught **chicken pox** instead. And believe me, I had had all the possible existing and non-existing diseases in the world BUT chicken pox! So I realized that yes, it was all new for me, even the illness and that no, I was not going to die. I was lucky, my Ameri-

can uncle was a doctor so he gave me some pills and I was ok. I was so ok that I could go to the Halloween party with my friends, but **I also had to dress up** and wear a mask. I found something in the house and I **pretended** I was a painter with colors all over me... not very original... but **it didn't matter! What mattered was being there**, going from house to house asking "**trick or treat**" like a real American girl. I was surprised looking in my basket at the end of the day, so full of sweets and chocolate and... small tubes of toothpaste!? Well, they gave us what they had.

10 December arrived, Christmas time. I was so excited to spend it there because in the States **it's a big deal**, so many lights, big trees everywhere and big parties too. I went to a beautiful place up in the mountains and we had a typical Christmas dinner there with all the family. I was waiting for their famous **stuffed** turkey and out it came... a huge turkey! We had fun, we ate a lot (as usual!) and we exchanged our gifts.

11 When I went back to school in January I started my Photography class and there I met the love of my life, at least so I thought. His name was Nathan, tall, handsome, hip-hop style, lovely smile, short curly dark hair. My heart would beat so fast each time I met him. One day we were in the dark room together, alone, developing our photos (no mobiles, no digital cameras at that time!) and he started to talk to me. I panicked. He said something I did not understand, I felt **deaf**. I asked him to repeat and I thought he said "So, Mary, what's your phone number?" and I said "439-4883". That was it, end of the conversation. I didn't notice there was a girl behind us, she came towards me and she **whispered** in my ear "He didn't ask for your phone number, he said 'what's your full name'". Uh. Ok. I just wanted to die right there and then, I wanted to disappear and cry.

12 I didn't eat that night, I never eat when **I have a crush on someone**, but it was a good thing because I was getting fatter and fatter... I didn't sleep either. The day after I was desperate and didn't want to go to school, but I had to. He was absent, **thank goodness**, so I didn't see him.

13 In the afternoon I came back home, I was sitting on my bed in my room and suddenly the phone rang... nothing strange **so far.** Then my American mom called me "Mary, **pick up** the phone!" Really? Ok. I picked up the phone and said "Hello?" and I just started to listen to the sound of a guitar and a sweet voice singing a beautiful romantic song. It was him, Nathan! I didn't know what to do, what to say, I was sitting there, a dumb look on my face, listening to this guy singing. Then he stopped and said "Like it? It's one of my favorite songs. **See**? I remembered your telephone number, sorry I didn't come to school today, I didn't feel very well. How are you, Mary?", well I just heard my name so I woke up from my **daydreaming** state of mind and I tried to say something "Hi, I'm ok, thanks. Beautiful song, you play very well". "Thank you. Would you like to go out sometime?" What did he just say?! Would I like to go out with him?! Of course! And I simply said "Yes". I wanted to answer "Yes I do, I want to marry you. But luckily enough I stopped at "yes". So we went out, he took me to the lake, so romantic, so nice. He played his guitar, he talked about his life, his family, his ambitions for the future, his dreams. And I listened, I was **staring** at him all the time like a stupid doll and then we kissed and then he asked me if I wanted to go to the **Prom** with him!

14 So there it was, my American dream! It wasn't success, money or peanut butter... it was love!

PRACTICE MAKES PERFECT

1. GOT IT? - Reading Comprehension

Answer the following questions.

1 • What word couldn't Mary understand when she arrived in America?

2 • What did she do with her friends in the woods?

3 • What was her favorite junk food?

4 • What difficult course did she take at school?

5 • Did she like it? Why/why not?

6 • What did she win at the fun fair?

7 • Why did she feel weak and sick?

8 • Who helped her when she got sick?

9 • What was the misunderstanding she had with Nathan?

10 • What did Nathan do when he called her?

2. IN OTHER WORDS

Try to reword the following expressions, finding a synonym(s).

1 I've just turned 40 = ...

1 tons of times = ...

4 Can you picture me there? = ...

8 We all became very close = ...

9 What mattered was being there = ...

3. KEY WORDS - Vocabulary

Match the word with its definition.

1	aware	to speak with a soft low voice
2	lazy	stupid
3	dumb	filled with something
4	to figure out	unhealthy food
6	adjust	clothes to be washed
6	laundry	adapt
8	fun fair	the opposite of a lively and active person
8	junk food	think, realize
9	pimple	a disease with marks on the skin
9	chicken pox	amusement park
9	to pretend	unable to hear
10	stuffed	a small spot on the skin
11	deaf	conscious of
11	to whisper	fantasize, dream with open eyes
13	daydreaming	looking at deeply, having a fixed look at something or someone
13	staring	to deceive, make believe, to put forward a false appearance

4. FIND THEM OUT! - Phrasal Verbs Crossword

There are a number of phrasal verbs used in the text. They can be found in the paragraphs indicated below. Find the phrasal verb, match the context with the crossword clue, then add the phrasal verbs (infinitive form) to complete the crossword.

Across

2. *To understand, to solve* (4)
4. *To let someone out of a vehicle at a particular location* (4)
6. *To stop, quit* (5)
8. *To be happy, brighten up* (7)
9. *To put formal clothes on for a special occasion, or to put a costume on* (9)
11. *To deal with a difficult situation* (4)

Down

1. *To go away from someone so that they are on their own* (4)
3. *Try to achieve, come on, you can do it!* (7)
5. *To discover* (6)
7. *To lift something* (13)
10. *To appear* (4)

A BIT MORE...

IDIOMS/SLANG & MORE

The following idioms and expressions are used in the text, learn their meanings and try the exercise that follows.

Where is it?	What is it?	What does it mean?
6	safe and sound	sano e salvo. *Safe means "away from danger" and sound means "unharmed"*
7	to be good at something	*to be able to do something well* = essere bravo in qualcosa
7	can't stand something or someone	*when you don't like something or someone* = non sopportare qualcosa o qualcuno
9	it doesn't matter	*it's not important, it doesn't worry me* = non importa, non fa niente
10	it's a big deal	letteralmente: «è un grande affare», nel significato di «è una cosa grossa, impressionante». Più spesso utilizzato nella forma negativa: *it's not a big deal* = non è niente di grave/importante/rilevante
12	to have a crush on someone	*to like someone very much* = avere una cotta per qualcuno
12	thank goodness	un'esclamazione colloquiale per dire: «grazie al cielo, meno male»
13	see?	il verbo see usato nel significato di «vedi?», metaforicamente inteso
13	so far	Significa «fin qui», è comune sentire l'espressione: *so far so good* = fin qui tutto bene

5. LOST IN TRANSLATION?

Translate the following sentences.

1 • Il mio volo è partito in ritardo perché l'aereo era danneggiato, grazie al cielo non ero da solo e sono arrivato a casa sano e salvo!

2 • Ugo non è bravo in inglese, ma non fa niente, sa cucinare benissimo!

3 • All'inizio non lo sopportavo, poi ho preso una cotta per lui e l'anno prossimo ci sposiamo.

4 • Dai, su, non è una cosa grave! Sei stato licenziato, ma ti ha già chiamato un'altra azienda. Vedi? Sei fortunato! Guarda sempre il lato positivo.

5 • Abbiamo fatto un ottimo lavoro finora, sono tutti soddisfatti con i risultati raggiunti.

CULTURE SHOCK!
Something about American Culture...

7 Marshmallows and chocolate

È qualcosa di molto popolare, grigliare sul fuoco i marshmallow e mangiarli caldi con pezzetti di cioccolato sopra. Da provare!

8 Peanut butter cups

Sono delle merendine (se così si può dire) ultracaloriche fatte di burro di arachidi e cioccolato. Da evitare se vogliamo salvaguardare il nostro fegato!

9 Trick or treat?

È la frase tipica che si pronuncia a Halloween quando si bussa casa per casa per chiedere: «Dolcetto o scherzetto?».

13 Prom

È il ballo di fine anno del liceo, un *big deal* in America! Molti ragazzi noleggiano la *limo* (limousine) e *dress up* molto eleganti per questa occasione unica. Chi non ha visto almeno una scena del ballo di fine anno in un film americano? Ecco, quello.

FOCUS ON...

THOUGH

La parola *though* può avere diversi significati, può essere usata al posto di:
if = se, sebbene, nonostante
even if = anche se
but = ma, però

Esempi:
Though she's not very good at cooking, she always tries to cook healthy food for the children.
Sebbene lei non sia molto brava a cucinare, prova sempre a cucinare cibo salutare per i suoi bambini.
Even though he failed all his exams at school, he still thinks he knows everything.
Anche se è stato bocciato in tutti i suoi esami a scuola, pensa comunque di sapere tutto.

BUT

Ricorda che *but*, come in questo caso nel testo, può essere usato non solo nel significato di «ma» ma anche per dire «tranne, eccetto».

Esempio:
We've invited everyone to the party but Dave and Emy, they're on holiday. Abbiamo invitato tutti alla festa, tranne Dave ed Emy: sono in vacanza.

GRAMMAR TOPIC: COMPARATIVES & SUPERLATIVES

Getting fatter and fatter

È un uso particolare del comparativo di maggioranza per dire «sempre più... grasso» (in questo caso). Si forma così: **comparativo di maggioranza dell'aggettivo in questione + *and* + ripetizione dello stesso comparativo.**

A questo proposito ripassiamo rapidamente i comparativi e superlativi?
Ma sì! Eccoli:

A. Aggettivi brevi composti da una solo sillaba aggiungono:
-**ER** per il comparativo di maggioranza
-**EST** per il superlativo.

Lily is taller than George.
Lily è più alta di George.

Joanne is the shortest girl in the class.
Joanne è la ragazza più bassa della classe.

B. Aggettivi che finiscono con la lettera -**Y**,composti da una o più sillabe. La -**Y** diventa -**I**, poi si aggiunge -**ER** per il comparativo di maggioranza, -**EST** per il superlativo.

My room is tidier than yours.
La mia camera è più ordinata della tua.

Boxing day is the busiest shopping day of the year in the UK.
Boxing day (Santo Stefano) è il giorno di shopping più intenso dell'anno nel Regno Unito.

C. Aggettivi composti da due o piu' sillabe aggiungono
more per il comparativo di maggioranza,
the most per il superlativo

Math is more enjoyable than History.
Matematica è più divertente di storia.

Venice is the most impressive city I've ever visited.
Venezia è la città più emozionante che io abbia mai visitato.

D. Per il comparativo di uguaglianza invece la forma resta invariata per tutti gli aggettivi: **AS** + aggettivo + **AS**.

My new car is as big as the old one.
La mia nuova macchina è tanto grande quanto quella vecchia.

ECCEZIONI!
• Alcuni aggettivi hanno forme irregolari:
good, better, the best

bad, worse, the worst
far, further/farther, the furthest/farthest

• Alcuni aggettivi non seguono le regole delle sillabe, alcuni hanno più di una forma possibile:

simple, simpler, simplest
clever, cleverer, cleverest
polite, politer/more polite, politest/the most polite etc.

6. LOST IN TRANSLATION?

Translate the following sentences.

1 • Kris è la ragazza più bella di questo ufficio, ma non la più simpatica.

2 • La cosa migliore che puoi fare è chiamare tutti, tranne lui, così capirà che sei arrabbiata.

3 • Anche se questo esame era più facile dell'ultimo, Tom lo ha sbagliato lo stesso.

4 • La mia nuova cucina è grande come la sua, ma lei pensa comunque che la sua sia migliore.

5 • È l'uomo più gentile che io abbia mai incontrato, lo voglio sposare!

7. LOST IN TRANSLATION? MIX IT UP!

Translate the following text into English using some of the words and expressions you have discovered in this story.

Ho appena compiuto cinquant'anni, sto diventando sempre più vecchia... e anche un po' sorda! La gente sembra sempre sussurrare le parole e io non le capisco. Ma non mi arrendo e fingo di sorridere. Mio cugino era bravo a inventare nuovi motti, il mio preferito era: "Vestiti bene e stai su di morale!". Mi piacerebbe anche aggiungere "Mangia cibo spazzatura", fa niente se non è salutare, ogni tanto fa bene all'umore! Vedi? Posso rinunciare a tutto eccetto che alla mia ironia! Cinquant'anni e fin qui tutto bene, ci sono arrivata sana e salva.

American English

What a Holiday!

STORY 2

1 It was one of the hottest summers ever, Frank and Nick had just finished their first year of University, so they decided it was time to go on holiday together to celebrate the end of their school year.

2 And what a school year they had had! Frank **fell in love with** the French teacher: mission impossible, of course. Nick started to play basketball for a new team and a boy fell in love with him: mission impossible 2. They went to so many parties, **actually** they were the ones that organized the parties and **invited people over**! No doubt they had fun, but they also had to study very hard, they were not used to it, so they really **deserved** a vacation now!

3 They didn't know where to go, they thought about it for a long time... not really... ten minutes and Spain was their final destination. Frank had some cousins in Barcelona so he thought it would be easier to go there and stay with them, less money to spend. What a **scrooge**. Well, they were still students after all, so let's forgive them. Speaking about saving money, going by plane was too expensive of course, so they decided to go by car. Too bad there was just a little tiny detail: they did not have a car! Nick's mom agreed to **lend** them hers, it was a very old car anyway, they wouldn't have to worry too much about **messing it up**. They packed so much into the car it was as if they didn't intend to return! Actually they had planned to come back in two weeks. The car was so full and heavy that they had trouble getting it started and getting it to go. Not a good start! They finally left home, wearing **boardies** and **flip flops**... you never know what

you're going to find on the way, maybe a gorgeous beach or a pool... and hey, they were on holiday after all!

4 "Hey Nick, are you sure you want to drive all the way? It's going to be a long trip."
"Yes, **I don't mind**, don't worry. Please turn on the air conditioning, it's boiling!" Frank tried to turn it on, but...
"It doesn't work, Nick" he shouted.
"What do you mean 'it doesn't work'? That's crazy! We're going to die!" "Ok, calm down, you know I can always **sort things out** for you, I have brought a fantastic Spanish fan so I can cool you down while you drive, happy?"
"No. Where did you get a Spanish **fan** from anyway?!"
"My sister had one and I thought I'd bring it with us, on our trip, just **to feel 'in the mood**' for Spain. Barcelona, here we come!!"
Frank was a very active guy, very genuine, **naïve** and optimistic. Nick was very funny, creative, but much more polite and serious, a pretty calm boy and he always wanted to plan everything, everything had to be under control.
"So Frank, did you at least tell your cousins we're coming to visit?" "Of course... not!" Nick gave him a **weird** and angry look: "**You're joking, aren't you**?"
"Of course... not! Don't worry, I told my grandma and I'm sure she called them." "**A leopard never changes its spots**, you're the same old **scatterbrain**! Let's hope your grandma calls them." Then he added "I was thinking of not stopping too often so we can get there sooner, ok?" "Sure."

5 After being in the car for twenty minutes:
"Nick, I have to go to the restroom."
"What are you, a little girl?! Alright, I'll stop at the next gas station, I also need to put gas in the car."
So Nick stopped at the gas station and Frank went to the restroom. When Frank came back he found Nick **arguing with** the gas station attendant: "You have to give me more money", said the man.
"I'll try to explain one more time," said Nick, "it was 55 euros, I gave you 60 so you owe me 5 euros **change**."
"You only gave me 50 so YOU owe me 5! You foreigner!"

"Well, we actually live nearby..."
Frank **looked at** them both, then he said to the man: "Here's your 5 euros, go get an ice-cream, forgive my friend, he's a **penny-pincher**, sorry." "What..?!" Nick shouted, but before he could properly reply to that comment, Frank **dragged** him away and they went to the bar to get a sandwich.
"I'd like a hamburger, please" said Frank. "A hamburger?!" Nick interrupted him. "Are you crazy?? You don't eat meat, don't you remember?? You're a **veggie**!". Then whispering to the barman "Sorry, forgive my friend, he **lost his mind** after his girlfriend **dumped** him". He looked at Frank and said out loud "He'll have the soy soup instead, please", smiling at him as if he were dumb. Frank remained speechless.
As soon as they got back in the car, Nick said "We're **even** now, my friend."

6 After eight hours driving, Nick was getting tired and Frank fell asleep. It was a beautiful night, a gorgeous full moon up in the sky and the road was almost empty, except for a few trucks. They left the highway and went onto a secondary road.
All of a sudden Frank woke up screaming "Oh my God! The phone's ringing!"
"But we don't have a phone!" Nick said and started to **laugh his head off**! It was a song on the radio! A song that began with the sound of a phone ringing. Nick almost lost control of the car because he just couldn't stop laughing. Frank didn't get it at first, he was too sleepy but then he started to laugh too.

7 They were both awake now, talking about their school year, their friends, their ex-girlfriends... and the ones they wished were their girlfriends!
Nick was deeply in love with Mary, but she didn't know it and he was too shy to tell her. He actually tried to tell her once but he didn't plan everything properly in the way he wanted to, so he gave up and never had another chance, so **disappointing**. Frank instead was a **Don Juan** and was never really in love with anyone. To tell the truth, he fell in love once, three years ago but **she broke up with him**. Nick was right, he has lost his mind since

then, he got too hurt, too upset. They both remained silent and quiet for a while, thinking about their own love stories.

8 All of a sudden Frank shouted again: "Oh my God again! A UFO! Look!"
Nick couldn't see anything, he thought Frank was still dreaming or something.
"Look!" Frank insisted "Look at that **flashing light** moving towards us!".
Nick could now see it and he looked at it with his mouth wide open, worried and scared, he couldn't believe his eyes: "You're right! **It does seem like a UFO**!". He did not stop driving but slowed down a bit to look more carefully. Nobody was there, not a car, not a person, not a house, not a dog! So they decided to stop to take a picture and capture the phenomenon, so other people could see it and believe them. But as they got closer and closer to the light... they **burst out laughing hysterically**! **Guess what?** It was just a broken street light!

9 It was definitely time for a coffee, time for a break. But where? They were lost in the middle of nowhere, no gas station around, no bars. There was a house not far away, they could see it and they could hear some music and voices coming from it. They wanted **to ask for** some water or for a place to spend the night or at least a safe place where they could rest a little, even in their car.
They reached this big strange house and found a family having a big party with a lot of people, friends and relatives. Nick and Frank finally felt **relieved**, they were sure they would find hospitality and generosity...
"Who are you? What do you want?" said **a hunk of a man** who seemed to be the party's boss.
"We're just two friends, lost in the countryside, looking for some food and drink..." Nick said, "...and a toilet", Frank added.
"Uh, ok then. We can't give you any food, but you can use our toilet and drink some water from the kitchen."
"Thank you so much", said Nick and he started to go towards the house but the man stopped him "It's 20 euros each to use the toilet and to have the water."

“Whaaaaaaaaaat?!” Frank shouted, but Nick tried to calm him down and he was able to negotiate, 30 for both.

10 Time to go back to their car and find their way again. After twenty hours driving (!!!) they finally got to Barcelona, so tired they couldn't even see the road anymore, they didn't even realize it was already morning. Their first and only thought was a soft bed to lie down on. But as soon as they got to **Frank's cousins' house**, they were welcomed by one of them, Pedro: “Hola! How was your trip? Welcome to Spain!”. Nick tried to say something “We're very tir...”, but before he could even complete the sentence, Pedro took a brand new **dinghy**, put it on Nick's shoulders and said “I bought it for you guys! We'll have so much fun! Come on, it's a beautiful day, let's go to the beach! You're not tired, are you?! You're too young to rest!”.
Nick stayed **still**, with a hopeless look in his eyes, whispering to Frank: “Hey, wasn't this supposed to be our relaxing holiday?!”... No answer from Frank, so Nick turned, looked around and he couldn't see his friend anymore... then he looked closer at the car... Frank was **lying** down on the **hood**, sleeping!

PRACTICE MAKES PERFECT

1. GOT IT? - Reading Comprehension

Answer the following questions.

1 • Which year of University have Nick and Frank just finished?

2 • Which teacher did Frank fall in love with?

3 • Where did they choose to go on holiday and why?

4 • What problem did they have in the car?

5 • What happened at the gas station between Nick and the attendant?

6 • What did Frank eat at the bar? Why?

7 • Why did Frank scream in the car (the first time he did it)?

8 • What was it that they thought was a UFO?

9 • Did they have to pay to go to the toilet? How much?

10 • What happened when they arrived in Barcelona?

2. KEY WORDS - Vocabulary

Match the word with its definition.

2	to deserve	to give something to someone on condition that it will be returned
3	to lend	to pull something/someone slowly and with difficulty
3	boardies	an object you can wave with your hands to move the air around you when it's too hot
3	flip flop	bathing suit
4	fan	a flat sandal, usually used in the summer
4	naïve	a foolish person, someone who forgets things
4	weird	feeling glad, no more anxiety, no worries
4	scatterbrain	someone who doesn't eat meat
5	change (n.)	stationary, not moving
5	penny-pincher	strange
5	to drag	to be worthy of, to merit
5	veggie	innocent
5	to dump	something bright that keeps going on and off
7	disappointing	someone who cares about money too much
8	flashing light	the part at the front of a car, covering the engine
9	relieved	to leave, break up, let fall
10	dinghy	the money you give in return when someone paid you more than needed
10	still (adj.)	when something or someone has not met your expectations
10	hood	a small inflatable boat

3. GUESS - Phrasal Verbs

Guess and write the meaning of the following phrasal verbs.

Where is it?	Phrasal Verbs	Meaning
2	to fall in love with someone	
2	to invite someone over	
3	to mess it up	
4	to sort things out	
7	to break up with someone	

REMEMBER

5 **to argue with someone on/about something** = discutere con qualcuno di qualcosa.

Dal testo: *When Frank came back he found Nick arguing with the gas station attendant...*
Quando Frank tornò, trovò Nick che stava discutendo con il benzinaio.

5 **to look at** = sappiamo che significa «guardare», ma dopo la preposizione at significa «guardare qualcosa o qualcuno» (*to look at something or someone*).

Dal testo: *Frank looked at them both...*
Frank li ha guardati entrambi...

LOOK è un verbo superfraseologico, a seconda della preposizione che lo segue cambia completamente significato.

Per esempio:
to look for = cercare
to look after = avere cura di, prendersi cura di

9 **to ask for** = idem come sopra: *to ask for something* significa «chiedere qualcosa». È importante non dimenticare la preposizione *for*!

Ma attenzione: chiedere a qualcuno = *ask someone* (senza preposizione dopo *ask*!)

Dal testo: *They wanted to ask for some water...*
Volevano chiedere dell'acqua...

A BIT MORE...

IDIOMS/SLANG & MORE

The following idioms and expressions are used in the text, learn their meanings and try the exercise that follows.

Where is it?	Idiom/Slang	Meaning
3	scrooge	*a person that cares about his own money too much, not generous* = tirchio, avaro
4	I don't mind!	*I don't care, it's ok* = non m'importa, non mi pesa
4	to feel 'in the mood'	*to feel right for that situation at that moment* = sentirsi dell'umore giusto per qualcosa
4	a leopard never changes its spots	*a person never really changes his/her habits and the way he/she is* = il lupo perde il pelo ma non il vizio
5	to lose one's mind	*to go crazy* = perdere la testa
6	to laugh one's head off	*to laugh a lot* = morire dal ridere
7	Don Juan	*a hot lover!* = un Don Giovanni, un latin lover!
8	to burst out laughing hysterically	*to start laughing in a loud way* = scoppiare a ridere fragorosamente
8	guess what?	indovina! Sai cosa? Sai che c'è?
9	a hunk of a man	*a handsome man* = un bel fusto, un gran pezzo d'uomo

4. LOST IN TRANSLATION?

Translate the following sentences.

1 • Sai che c'è? Se mi lasci sono felice perché sei sempre stato un taccagno! Come ho fatto a innamorarmi di te?

2 • Li ho invitati a casa, così portano Steve che un è bel fusto e lo posso presentare a mia cugina.

3 • Se potessi indosserei le infradito tutto il giorno, anche al lavoro, invece posso solo portarmi un ventaglio.

4 • Non so cosa sia successo, ma ho perso la testa e ho fatto un casino. Ho mangiato una bistecca, ma sono vegetariana!

5 • Mi sento sollevata, i miei sei figli stanno guarendo dall'influenza.

6 • Mio fratello è così ingenuo che non discute mai con nessuno di niente.

CULTURE SHOCK!
Ae vs Be - American English vs British English

Ae	Be	Meaning
vacation	holiday	vacanza
truck	lorry	camion
highway	motorway	autostrada
hood	bonnet	cofano
gas	petrol	benzina
gas station	petrol station	distributore di benzina
to realize	to realise	realizzare
to organize	to organise	organizzare

FOCUS ON...

ACTUALLY (2)

Ebbene esistono (e sono tanti) i **false friends** in inglese, cioè quelle parole che sembra abbiano lo stesso significato che in italiano ma invece no!
actually = in realtà, in effetti
currently = attualmente
Esempio:
I'm currently staying at the Hilton in New York.
(*currently*, **non** *actually*!)
Attualmente alloggio presso l'Hilton a New York.

YOU'RE JOKING, ARENT YOU? (4)

Ricordi cosa sono le **question tags**, vero?
Ecco, servono proprio a rendere in inglese quel "vero?" italiano.
Si formano mettendo il verbo ausiliare della frase principale nella sua forma opposta + il soggetto della frase.
Qualche esempio:
You're sure, aren't you?
Sei sicuro, vero?
She's the new student, isn't she?
Lei è una nuova studentessa, vero?
They work on Saturdays, don't they?
Lavorano il sabato, vero?

WATCH OUT!
Si fa un'**eccezione** quando il soggetto è **io**.
I'm leaving at 9.00 pm, **arent' I**?
Parto alle 9 di sera, vero?

IT DOES SEEM LIKE A UFO (8)

Gli ausiliari (*do/does/did* ecc.) si usano **solo** per formare frasi interrogative e negative in inglese. **Falso!** A volte si possono usare nelle frasi affermative per enfatizzare, sottolineare il concetto.

Nell'esempio:
It does seem like a UFO = sembra davvero/sembra proprio un UFO (does serve per evidenziare il fatto che sembrava proprio che fosse un UFO!)

EVEN (5)

We're even now, my friend. Siamo pari ora, amico mio.

... so tired they couldn't even see the road anymore.
... così stanchi che non riuscivano neanche a vedere più la strada.

Even in queste frasi ha due significati diversi: nella prima ha funzione di **aggettivo** (= siamo pari), nella seconda ha funzione di **avverbio** (= neanche, perfino).

LYING (10)

Dal verbo *to lie*, ricorda che il dittongo (cioè due vocali vicine) **IE** diventa **Y** quando aggiungo **ING**!

Esempio: il verbo *to die* diventa *dying* nella forma in -ING.

GRAMMAR TOPIC: POSSESSIVE S (Genitivo Sassone)

Il genitivo sassone, cioè "apostrofo + s" sul nome del possessore, serve per esprimere, appunto, possesso, ovvero per indicare **di chi è qualcosa**. È usato per persone e animali; se invece si tratta di cose/oggetti si usa la preposizione **of**.

Vediamo qualche esempio:
Tommy's watch is broken. L'orologio di Tommy è rotto.
My dog's food is special. Il cibo del mio cane è speciale.
I don't remember the title of the book. Non ricordo il titolo del libro.

Ricorda che ai nomi plurali regolari che finiscono con una -S si aggiunge **solo** l'apostrofo!

Come nell'esempio preso dalla nostra storia:

10 *Frank's cousins' house.* La casa dei cugini di Frank.

Se invece finisce con -S un nome proprio di persona allora vale la regola standard: si aggiunge "apostrofo + s" al nome proprio.

Ross's hair is black. I capelli di Ross sono neri.

ECCEZIONI!
A. Con i nomi di cosa quando esprimono temporalità:
Tomorrow's meeting is very important. L'incontro di domani è molto importante.
B. Con i nomi di nazione o città:
London's museums are beautiful. I musei di Londra sono belli.

5. LOST IN TRANSLATION?

Translate the following sentences using the "Focus on" and "Grammar" topics.

1 • L'incontro di domani è alle 7.00 del mattino. Mi passi a prendere, vero?

2 • Mio zio vince sempre quando giochiamo a carte, ma finalmente ora siamo pari.

3 • Il figlio del cugino di mio padre vive a Madrid.

4 • «A che ora torni domani?» «Beh, in realtà... non parto più!»

5 • Lei porta sì gli occhiali! Sono sicura, sono gialli!

6 • Il Duomo di Milano è stupendo, ma preferisco la Sagrada Familia a Barcellona.

7 • Non riesco a ricordare il nome della via dove si trova la casa di Mike, e tu?

ABOUT PRONUNCIATION

-ED - Queste due semplici lettere possono dare parecchi problemi, soprattutto alla fine di una parola, anzi di un verbo! Eppure le regole sono semplici:

-ED = ID: quando un verbo finisce per -T o -D (o un suono corrispondente)
-ED = T: quando un verbo finisce per -SS, -PP, -SH, -CH, -X, -K (o un suono corrispondente)
-ED = D (la E è muta): in tutti gli altri casi!

Valgono le stesse regole per gli aggettivi che finiscono in -ED, anche se qualcuno fa naturalmente **eccezione**! I seguenti aggettivi, infatti, sono i "ribelli fuori dal gruppo" e la loro -ED si pronuncia ID, anche se non finiscono né con -T né con -D:

blessed = benedetto
crooked = storto, disonesto
dogged = ostinato
learned = colto
naked = nudo
ragged = logoro, stracciato
wicked = cattivo
wretched = orribile
aged = invecchiato, stagionato (questo aggettivo fa doppia eccezione perché si può pronunciare sia con D sia con ID)

6. PRONUNCIATION EXERCISE

Ora che sai le regole, ecco una lista di verbi in -ED presi dal testo. Prova a scrivere la pronuncia corretta accanto. E non ti arrendere, la lista continua, trova tutti i verbi in ED nella storia e continua a esercitarti!

Verb	Pronunciation	Verb	Pronunciation
finished		tried	
decided		shouted	
started		called	
organized		added	
invited		stopped	
used		looked	
deserved		dragged	
agreed		interrupted	
packed		remained	
planned		wished	

Ae
American English

A Sleepless Night

STORY 3

1 It's 3 am and I'm still awake. You might think I'm at the disco or at a party drinking with friends, maybe flirting with that beautiful girl I met a week ago. **Nope**, none of that. I simply had lasagna for dinner! I should never have listened to my uncle Eric "Come on, big man! Have some more lasagna!" First of all, "big man" is not just a nickname, I am actually a big man...quite fat indeed! Some people say that fat is good, they say it shows you're healthy and rich and that fat people are usually funnier than **skinny** ones...how can I not agree? But unfortunately I'm not rich at all, nor healthy (funny? Well, at least I hope so). My uncle is from France, but he married an Italian woman. She convinced him Italy is better in so many ways and he believed her, he probably had no choice but to ask for a divorce.
So we now all call him uncle Tony, after the name of our favorite Italian restaurant in town. I remember when my Swedish friend came to visit me last year and uncle Tony invited us for dinner, he loves cooking and he's very good at it. My friend is a very nice girl, always **smiling**, happy and **cheerful**, she enjoys Italian food very much. We were there, sitting at the dinner table, **tasting** this amazing lasagna (yes, again!), when my uncle asked my friend "Sasha, you're always so happy, what's your secret?" Sasha said "Prozac!" and she started to laugh. Uncle Tony started to laugh too, but not for the same reason... he thought Sasha said "Prosecc", meaning Prosecco, the Italian wine! It was so funny, I'm still smiling now just thinking about it!

2 So let's come back to reality, here I am, **doubled up** in pain, thinking that maybe some Prosecco now would help me digest that lasagna! I give up on the idea of getting some sleep and turn on

the TV, looking for some boring channel that could relax me a bit. But I find a thriller instead. I decide to watch it for a while but I can't take it anymore and **switch the TV off** and the computer on. "I could work for a bit", I think. I open my work files, but after ten minutes I start talking to myself about the Stock Market and I feel **kind of nuts**, so I stop. I need to relax, let's write an e-mail to the love of my life. She still doesn't know it, but I love her deeply and completely, her name is Maggie and **I fell head over heels**. It was **love at first sight**, I write a letter to her every day, but I've never sent one.

"Dear Maggie, Here I am again, thinking of you as I always do. I can't sleep tonight and your face is all I have in mind.

I know your life is already so busy and **stuffed** with problems and I'm certainly not in the picture, but I don't care, I just want to have the chance to see you every day, even if it's just for a few minutes, the time for a coffee or a chat. I love your hair, so blonde and curly, your greeny-blue eyes, your long smooth legs... not sure about the **smooth** part, never touched them, but I'm sure they are. You're my only wish each time I see a falling star (which happens very rarely anyway). You're the only reason I would put on some clothes and leave this house now, even though I'd rather stay here half **naked** with you in my arms.

Sometimes I wonder if you feel the same way about me...

With all my love, Mike" I was never so good at writing romantic stuff, but she inspires me.

3 I wake up after two hours, I fell asleep on the chair in front of my computer, very comfortable indeed. I **rush** to the bathroom, wash my face and **get dressed** in less than seven minutes, a record for the year. I go out, slam the door, forget to lock it and start running. I get to work at 8.03 am, three minutes late. "Mike, come on! Your boss is not in the mood today, you'd better hurry!" my colleague said.

8.05 am, I sit at my desk and look at her. "Mike, you're late again. We have that very important meeting today at 6 o'clock, remember? I expect the very best from you and your presentation." Do I remember? Of course... yes, the meeting... oh no! My presentation? My presentation! Where is it? Where did I put it? Can't find it, it's nowhere. What can I do now, just improvise? Not that I'm

bad at it, but this meeting is too important and I can't disappoint my boss: I'm a dead man, **wish me luck**.
It's 5 pm, I'm still looking for the presentation or at least something I can **grab hold of**, something that will enable me to survive this nightmare. I call uncle Tony and ask him to prepare some food for our clients at work, I want them to waste some time before the meeting so I'll have more time to collect my thoughts and **make something up**.
5.30 pm, uncle Tony comes with the food, pretending he's from a catering company, even if everybody knows him at work. My boss gives me a **puzzled** look but I immediately smile and say "I thought it would be nice to offer our guests some specialties, to make a good impression", and she smiled back, a fake smile but still a smile.
5.45 pm, the attendees arrive and I have no more time to waste, I feel hopeless and I decide to tell the truth, but as I go towards my boss, she says "Mike, you always forget! I did something for you again! I sent your e-mail with your presentation to everybody, so they can see it while you explain your plan." "But how..." she **walked away fast** and didn't give me the chance to say: "But how is that possible?! I lost the presentation, I never sent it to you!". I start feeling **scared**, but I also have to start saying something. I always start my speeches with some funny stories to get their attention. When I finish my introduction, my boss interrupts for a second and says "I sent Mike's presentation to all of you, please open it and feel free to ask any questions at the end, thank you." After a couple of minutes I look at my **audience** (90% men), some of them are **laughing hysterically**, some seem annoyed. I look at my boss, hoping for some sort of explanation, but she can't understand either... until she opens the file she sent, the one she thought my presentation was attached to. She starts reading, whispering "Dear Maggie...". She doesn't even look at me, she runs away, out of the room, I go after her, trying to stop her "Maggieeee!". She disappeared. I come back to apologize to the people in the meeting room, I suggest that they enjoy the food and go back to their office, the meeting **has been officially put off** to **who knows** when. Right now, if I could, I would put off my whole life too. Of course, the whole building now knows, everybody is giving me a sarcastic smile, this is

much worse than I expected. Only Rob, my colleague and friend, says a few words of comfort (at least he tries): "Hey Mike, **don't sweat the small stuff**, come on, it's just an e-mail and **it could be any Maggie**, it doesn't mean it has to be Maggie your boss!". "Rob, thanks, but it's not working, **I screwed up**."

4 **She had never taken any days off** before. She took a month. A month? It seemed a bit **over the top** to me, I needed to talk to her. She won't answer my phone calls, e-mails, knocks at her door. I'd had enough, I was the humiliated one, **if anything**, she should be flattered! I won't give up on her and as **my French-Italian-whatever uncle** taught me, I swear **I'll win her over**, let's start **charming** her.

5 The day after I decide to buy her favorite flowers, daisies. I leave them in front of her house since she won't talk to me, but when I come back in the evening they're still there and it's not a good **sign** I suppose. What was I thinking? Flowers? To her? The big manager, the big woman (metaphorically speaking in her case, of course). I need something else to attract her, but I have no inspiration because I honestly think she doesn't care for me at all. I realize I'm sitting on her doorsteps when suddenly the front door opens, her hand throws a letter to me as **if it were** a bone for a dog. Well, I really must have looked like a dog in her eyes, sitting here, waiting for a sign from my owner, but the sign actually arrived! I was so thrilled, so excited, I got something from her at last and hey, maybe she has confessed her love to me with this letter. **I open it up** "I can't go out with one of my employees, it's written in my contract, so please just leave me alone." Well, that is what I call a real confession of... rejection. Ok then, got it, no problem, I'll go back to my old life.

6 When Maggie came back to work after a month, she didn't find me there anymore and she didn't even ask for any additional information, they said I **resigned**, **period**. It was Christmas time and I knew they had a very important meeting before the holidays, as usual. I also knew they would have a party at the end of it to celebrate. I planned everything with great care, it will be a real surprise. She welcomed the guests, the meeting went

well, they were all happy with the company results, new clients smiled and shook hands. "Enjoy the food now and thank you all" she ended. And here we come, my uncle and I, the catering guys, ready with food and drinks. She surely didn't expect to see me there, surely not serving food. But there I was, trying to look good, a waiter wearing a **tuxedo**. She looked shocked, I got closer, "I'm not one of your employees anymore, **honey**" and **I kept on serving**. I had changed my life, decided to **start up** a catering company together with uncle Tony and we **were doing a roaring trade**, the only thing that **bothered** me was that I was getting fatter, but it didn't matter because **I had also taken up** boxing... I had **to work off** my anger somehow! I left a note on her desk at the end of the event "MEET ME IN CLACTON PARK AT 7 pm TOMORROW." I didn't ask her, I wanted her there, she had to come.

7 7.00 pm today, I'm waiting.
7.30 pm, still waiting, but it's normal, isn't it? She's a woman after all.
8.00 pm, I'm **chilly** but still here, hopeful.
8.15 pm, "I'm sorry Mike, you won't believe it, but I was ready at 6.30 then my grandma called, she hurt her knee so I had to call my mom, but she didn't have a car, so I had to go **pick her up**, we went to my grandma's, then I got an urgent phone call from the office then...". I shut her mouth with my index finger:
"Please stop, it's ok! I'm still here."
"Ok, thanks", she started to look down (not a good sign), "I just wanted to say..." "Maggie, I know it seems **crazy** but **YOU're driving me crazy**! We've been working together for five years, I never said a word about my feelings, but I love you, even though you're a bit **tough** at work and they call you "**the psycho**" because you're so **moody**..." "What?! I didn't know that!"
"Please don't interrupt, I wouldn't focus on the word "psycho" if I were you but on the word "love"... I know you're a good person, you're special to me, I not only know your strengths, but also and above all I know your weaknesses and I love you just the way you are ... want me to sing it for you?" I smiled. But she didn't smile back. "You see, Mike, no offence, you're a great man, I mean it, but I'm **engaged**." "Engaged?! But you've always said you were single, no man beside you ever!" "That's because it's

someone from the office and I didn't want anybody to know till it was official, till now." "Someone from the office?? Who? Please tell me, I need to know." "Maybe it's better if..."
"Please, Maggie, you owe me this at least, who's your **fiancé**?"
"It's Rob." And **I passed out**, **I was out like a light**.
I woke up at her place, she was holding a glass of something in her hands and I opened my eyes thinking I was having a bad dream, she was my wife and we would live happily now and forever. "How do you feel, Mike? Are you ok? I'm sorry I hurt your feelings." The word "hurt" made me realize it wasn't a bad dream. "I'm ok, I just don't understand... Rob? He's one of my best friends at the office..." "I know but we didn't know how to tell you, so..." Someone was at the door, Rob came in: "Hi there, Mike. It's me...". "Yes, it's you, "**buddy**"! It's YOU!" I suddenly got up and I almost jumped on him, but I **slipped** and fell.
"Mike, I really care about you, but I love Maggie, how could I choose between love and friendship? Please try to understand..."
"At least you could have told me!" and I left, slamming the door on the way out.

8 I went to my uncle's, my only refuge, the only honest person on earth, the only one... "Uncle Tony! What are you doing with Sasha??" I found them on the sofa, kissing. "Mike, don't be so shocked! You know that your aunt and I divorced a long time ago and Sasha came back to visit, she's got some fantastic Swedish **recipes** to teach me!"
Now what? My dad is a super hero and my mom Catwoman and I never knew?! I guess I'll go home and get some sleep.

9 A year goes by... It's 3 am and I'm still awake. You might think I'm at the disco or at a party drinking with friends, maybe flirting with that beautiful girl I met a week ago. Nope, none of that. I'm simply serving food at Maggie and Rob's wedding reception, together with my uncle and Sasha, my dear Swedish friend. And this is my life. Wait, is it really? It can't be, where's the happy ending and all that? Well, I've already got my eyes on that girl over there, dark hair, blue eyes... she **winked**, she must be crazy about me already.

PRACTICE MAKES PERFECT

1. GOT IT? - Reading Comprehension

Answer the following questions.

1 • What does Mike think about fat people?

2 • Where does Mike's uncle come from?

3 • What is Mike's uncle's nickname? Where does it come from?

4 • What is the misunderstanding between uncle Tony and Sasha?

5 • Why does Mike feel sick and in pain?

6 • What does Mike do after he turns off the computer?

7 • What does uncle Tony have to do for Mike's meeting and why?

8 • How does Mike usually start his presentations? Why?

9 • What does Mike do after reading Maggie's letter?

10 • How long have Mike and Maggie been working together?

11 • Why did Mike pass out?

2. KEY WORDS - Vocabulary

Look at the definitions below, can you find the word in the text that matches with the given meaning?

1 very thin

1 happy

1 to test the flavor of something by eating or drinking

2 crazy

2 filled with something

2 free from hair, not rough

2 nude, with no clothes

3 to hurry

3 confused

3 the people present at a meeting/conference

4 to please someone by compliments or attention

6 to quit/give up your job

6 man's formal dress

6 to annoy, to cause someone trouble

7 cold

7 not soft, strong, hard, difficult

7 a person that often changes his/her feelings (happy, sad, etc.)

7 to plan to get married

7 more than just a boyfriend/girlfriend, someone who is due to get married

7 to slide

9 to close and open one eye quickly, it is often done as a signal

3. FIND THEM OUT! - Phrasal Verbs Crossword

There are a number of phrasal verbs used in the text. They can be found in the paragraphs indicated below. Find the phrasal verb, match the context with the crossword clue, then add the phrasal verbs (infinitive form) to complete the crossword.

Across

4. *To make something become open* (5)
6. *To persuade someone to support or want you* (4)
8. *To ruin* (3)
9. *To postpone* (3)
11. *To invent* (3)
13. *To get rid of, eliminate* (6)
14. *To stop something from functioning* (2)
15. *To bend over in pain* (2)

Down

1. *To begin a new project/business* (6)
2. *To take something in your hands quickly* (3)
3. *To start a new hobby/activity* (6)
5. *To get someone (in the car) and take them somewhere* (7)
7. *To continue* (6)
10. *To not work for a period of days* (4)
12. *To faint, lose consciousness temporarily* (7)

A BIT MORE...

IDIOMS/SLANG & MORE

The following idioms and expressions are used in the text; learn their meanings and try the exercise that follows.

Where is it?	What is it?	What does it mean?
1	nope	è un'espressione che si usa in un inglese colloquiale, molto informale, al posto del semplice "no"
2	I fell head over heels	*intensely, completely*. Di solito è accostato al concetto di innamoramento, come in questo caso, «mi sono innamorato perdutamente»
2	love at first sight	amore a prima vista
3	wish me luck	quando qualcuno chiede a qualcun altro di augurargli «buona fortuna». Se invece sei tu a voler augurare «buona fortuna» a qualcuno allora dirai semplicemente *good luck*! Comune è anche l'espressione *break a leg*, più spesso usata prima di uno spettacolo teatrale o un esame/evento importante
3	laughing hysterically	ridere a crepapelle
3	who knows	chissà
3	don't sweat the small stuff	non ingigantire le cose
4	over the top	un po' troppo, un po' esagerato
4	if anything	per dire «se proprio, semmai», come in questo caso: «io ero quello umiliato, semmai ce ne fosse uno» ecc..
4	my French-Italian-whatever uncle	questo *whatever* indica che lo zio ha diverse nazionalità ed è inteso come «qualsivoglia, qualunque». *Whatever* è anche un intercalare nell'inglese colloquiale, nello slang: esprime indifferenza, ha significato di «fai come vuoi, fai come ti pare, pazienza, amen»
6	period	qui inteso come «punto, fine, stop». Letteralmente significa la fine di un paragrafo.

Where is it?	What is it?	What does it mean?
6	honey	letteralmente «miele», usato comunemente come nomignolo affettuoso inteso come «tesoro, caro»
6	do a roaring trade	ovvero *to do good business*, *to sell well/quickly*, un'attività prospera, fiorente
7	YOU're driving me crazy!	tu mi stai facendo impazzire!
7	the psycho	un modo informale e abbreviato per dire «psicopatico»
7	I was out like a light	*in a deep sleep*: svenire, crollare, perdere i sensi
7	buddy	*friend*, un modo informale per dire «amico», molto usato nel linguaggio colloquiale

4. LOST IN TRANSLATION?

Translate the following sentences.

1 • Jack si è innamorato perdutamente di me, sono lusingata ma non è stato amore a prima vista per me. Credo che inventerò una scusa per lasciarlo.

2• Lisa è davvero bellissima, mi ha fatto l'occhiolino e mi ha sedotto! Siamo fidanzati ora e ci sposiamo a giugno del 2030.

3• «Ho appena iniziato golf, mi piace tantissimo.» «Non volevi fare tennis?» «Sì, ma l'insegnante era un po' lunatico, così ho rinunciato.»

4• «Devo sfogare la mia rabbia, ho deciso di licenziarmi, augurami buona fortuna.» «Per favore, non svenire davanti al tuo capo come fai sempre! Non puoi semplicemente prenderti qualche giorno libero come fanno tutti?»

5• «C'erano molti partecipanti alla conferenza, mi ero preparato un discorso molto importante, ma ho rovinato tutto! Avevo troppa ansia e ho iniziato a balbettare.» «Amico, dai, non ingigantire le cose, sono certo che non hanno pensato fossi pazzo ma solo molto timido.»

6• «Mi dispiace disturbarti, ma mio marito vorrebbe assaggiare la tua famosa torta al cioccolato. Puoi darmi la ricetta per favore?» «Certo, nessun problema! Non sapevo che gli piacessero i dolci, è pelle e ossa!» «Hai ragione, chissà come fa a non metter su peso!»

FOCUS ON...

PRONUNCIATION

SIGHT vs LAUGH (2)

Ci sono diversi modi per pronunciare le due consonanti GH. In questo contesto troviamo due parole molto differenti tra loro. Nella prima, *sight*, GH è muto e non si pronuncia (= *sait*). Nella seconda parola invece, *laugh*, GH si pronuncia come la lettera F (= *laf*).

NAKED (2)

Fa parte di quegli aggettivi che fanno eccezione: la -ED finale si pronuncia ID e non T come la regola vorrebbe (= *neikid*).

SIGN vs SIGNATURE (5)

Anche GN è un suono particolare in inglese e può avere varie sfaccettature. Per esempio, nella parola *sign* è muto (= *sain*), mentre nella parola *signature* si pronuncia con suono gutturale GN.

PSYCHO (7)

La "P" è muta = *saiko*

RECIPES (8)

Si pronuncia *rèsepiz*, la pronuncia è un po' diversa dallo spelling della parola!

CHALLENGE TIME

Can you find other words with the same pronunciation as the words above? Think about it and give some examples.

3 Get dressed

Ricorda che il verbo GET ha tanti significati e può essere usato in molti modi, in particolare, come nell'esempio del testo, serve per fare la forma riflessiva del verbo.

Esempi:

get dressed = vestirsi
get married = sposarsi
get lost = perdersi
get wet = bagnarsi
get dry = asciugarsi
get nervous = agitarsi, preoccuparsi, innervosirsi
get mad/angry = arrabbiarsi
get bored = annoiarsi
get tired = stancarsi
get close = avvicinarsi

3 It could be any Maggie

L'unico caso in cui si può usare *any* nelle frasi affermative è quando assume il significato di «qualsiasi, qualunque».

Esempio:

The candies are on the table, you can take any (of them).
Le caramelle sono sul tavolo, puoi prenderne una qualsiasi.

5 If it were

Ricorda che dopo **if** il verbo "essere" al passato è **were** per tutte le persone, anche se nell'inglese moderno attuale è accettato (e quindi corretto) anche *was* per la prima e la terza persona singolare (*I*, *he*, *she*, *it*).

Esempio:

If I were you I would call her and tell her she's a liar.
Se fossi in te la chiamerei e le direi che è una bugiarda.

GRAMMAR TOPIC:
HAD BETTER & WOULD RATHER

You'd better = you HAD BETTER

Si usa la costruzione HAD BETTER quando si vuole dare un consiglio o un suggerimento in modo deciso, convinto, per dire a qualcuno cosa deve fare, cosa sarebbe meglio che facesse.

> Si usa di solito la forma abbreviata **'d better**.
> È una costruzione verbale usata sempre e solo al passato, **non** si può dire *have better*, ma solo **HAD better**, con la forma di *have* al passato.
> Esiste anche alla forma negativa: *had better not*.

Non è mai seguito dal *to* ma direttamente dalla forma base del verbo, come nell'esempio preso dal testo: *you'd better hurry* = faresti meglio a sbrigarti.

Esempio:
You'd better turn off the TV and do your homework before your mom gets angry.
Faresti meglio a spegnere la TV e fare i compiti prima che tua mamma si arrabbi.

She'd better not cook meat tonight, I'm a vegetarian.
Farà meglio a non cucinare carne stasera, sono vegetariano.
Nota come *had better* sia un consiglio, ma dato in modo perentorio, deciso, diverso per esempio dall'uso di un consiglio dato usando il modale *should*.

Prova a confrontare queste frasi:
You should go to the doctor if you don't feel well. Dovresti andare dal medico se non stai bene. (consiglio, suggerimento generico)

You'd better go to the doctor, you've had headache for a month!
Faresti meglio ad andare dal medico, hai mal di testa da un mese! (consiglio che suona quasi come un obbligo, devi necessariamente andare dal medico, non puoi più farne a meno)

Questa forma può essere usata anche come risposta breve, per enfatizzare la risposta stessa, per esempio:

"Shall I finish this work by Monday?" "You'd better!"
«Dovrei finire questo lavoro entro lunedì?» «Faresti meglio!»

A volte, nel linguaggio colloquiale e informale, si omette *had* e si usa solo *better*, ma il significato resta lo stesso:
I better go now = I'd better go now = Farei meglio ad andare ora.

Spesso si confonde questa forma verbale con l'espressione *would rather*, che, oltre alla forma, ha un significato diverso. Come *had better*, anche *would rather* è seguito sempre dal verbo in forma base e mai dal *to* ed è spesso usato nella forma abbreviata **'d rather** (o, per le negative, **'d rather not**). Da qui forse nasce la confusione, ma quella 'd apostrofata in questo caso sta per *would*, non *had*! Anche il significato è diverso, come abbiamo detto:
would rather = would prefer to = preferire.

Esempi:
I'd better wash my car, but I'd rather go shopping.
Farei meglio a lavare l'auto, ma preferirei andare a fare shopping.

Would you rather stay with uncle Tom or uncle Nick?
Preferiresti stare con zio Tom o con zio Nick?

5. LOST IN TRANSLATION?

Translate the following sentences.

1 • In qualunque posto io vada mi perdo sempre e devo fermarmi a chiedere indicazioni perché non ho il navigatore sulla mia vecchia macchina.

2 • Se fossi in lui mi arrabbierei molto, avrebbero dovuto sposarsi tra due giorni e lei lo ha lasciato!

3 • Sta piovendo, faresti meglio a non bagnarti o ti verrà ancora l'influenza!

4 • Preferirei non uscire stasera, domani mattina devo alzarmi molto presto, ho un incontro importante al lavoro.

5 • Farebbe bene ad andare alla festa di Patty, anche se preferirebbe cenare con noi perché ho fatto il suo piatto preferito.

6. LOST IN TRANSLATION? MIX IT UP!

Translate the following text into English using some of the words and expressions you have discovered in this story.

Io e mio fratello abbiamo avviato un nuovo business, vendiamo abbigliamento sportivo online. Abbiamo creato un fantastico sito web e stiamo vendendo molto! Chissà se avrà sempre così successo, speriamo di sì. Incontriamo tanta gente per lavoro perché abbiamo bisogno di comprare i prodotti e discutere il costo. Ho incontrato questa ragazza bellissima e intelligente l'altro giorno, mi sta facendo impazzire, penso sempre a lei. Grazie a lei non mi annoio mai al lavoro e trovo sempre una scusa per chiamarla. Mio fratello dice che è una psicopatica solo perché cambia spesso umore ma io penso che questo è semplicemente il modo in cui sono fatte tutte le ragazze. Potrei avere qualsiasi ragazza ma io voglio solo lei. Se fossi più coraggioso, le scriverei una lettera d'amore, anche se è fuori moda. «Faresti meglio ad attenerti al lavoro e dimenticare quella ragazza», questo è quello che continua a dirmi mio fratello. A lui non piace, pensa sia pelle e ossa, ma a me non importa, abbiamo gusti differenti. Squilla il telefono: «Ti disturbo?» sento la sua voce parlare, che bella voce... «Naturalmente no! Tu non mi disturbi mai.»

«Volevo solo dirti che ho deciso di dare le dimissioni, ho trovato un lavoro migliore. È stato bello lavorare con te e ti auguro il meglio.»

«Ehm, ok, ma faresti bene a venire a trovarmi prima di licenziarti.»

"Così, questa è la fine" pensai. "Preferirei passare il resto della mia vita in prigione se non posso vederla più! Sto impazzendo, devo assolutamente vederla." Ed eccoci qui, due anni dopo, felicemente sposati.

American English

A Dog's Life

STORY 4

1 When you're a child they often ask you "What do you want to do when you **grow up**?" I always answered "Detective!", but I work in a bank, **a nine-to-five job**, no excitement but not too much stress either. On an ordinary day, while I was going back home on the subway as usual, at about 5.30 pm, my cell phone rings but I don't even have time to say "Hello" before I hear my name being screamed "Booooooooooooooooooob!"

"Linda what happened?! Are you ok?!"

"No, I'm not ok! They took Arthur, they took him!" "Ok, **calm down**, breathe, I'm on my way." I always wanted to be an investigator, this was my chance to show what I could do.

I get to my sister's house after about an hour (I always told her to move closer but she never wanted to, so **stubborn**), I ring the doorbell but nobody answers. I call her on the phone "I'm here, where are you?" "**Comin'**." I see her coming closer, running towards me, **out of breath**, hugging a bag of dry dog food. "I've lost Arthur, I'm **frantic** with worry, someone has taken him!" She screams. I put my hand over her mouth, tell her to calm down and we go into her house. "Linda, OK, let's start from the beginning. Tell me everything in the order it happened and give me as many details as you can." "OK, I'll try. Last night, Arthur was here with us ..." and she starts **whining** again... and I stop her again, "Linda! That's enough! I said calm down! He's just a dog after all!" I **regretted** saying that as soon as I'd said it, she looks at me in disgust, I feel like she would kill me if she could, but she just insults me: "Typical! Cynical as always! You don't understand, Arthur is like a son to me."

Sister-brother relationships are hard work, but I know I have a natural talent for it so I try to repair the damage I've just caused:

"Linda, OK, I'm a cynical, superficial and immoral person, but now I'm really interested in finding Arthur, but if you can't tell me what happened I can't help you." I convince her, at last.
"I took him for a walk in the park after dinner, we came back after about an hour, then we went to bed."
"Where was your husband?" "I know you don't like him, but you could at least call him by name! Andy was with us, but he went to bed earlier, he's gone to Paris this morning on business, he had an early flight." "So we can't **report** him, uh? Too bad!" I say, laughing **to downplay** it a bit, even if I really thought it, **what a pity** not to be able to **blame** him. He's a good man, but **he always pokes fun at people**, he often lies just to be sarcastic or simply to do what he really wants to. "No, Bob, we can't blame him! However, this morning, as I was saying, we both went out early, but Arthur was here, in our living room, awake and ready to have his favorite **biscuits**. I left the house before Andy because there's so much traffic in the morning and **it takes me forever to get to work**." "I always wonder why you don't take the subway, it's so much more **convenient** and relaxing." "Relaxing?! It's always so **crowded**, it smells and I can't breathe, anyway, are you listening to me? **Who cares** about the subway?!"
"Yes, yes, OK, you're right, sorry." My sister has only taken the subway a couple of times in her life, when she was forced to by her teachers for a school trip. She always **avoided** public transport, can't stand it, she'd rather go by helicopter than take the bus or use the subway! She even hates taxis... she's **paranoid**! She wanted to be a writer, an artist, but then, just like me, **she ended up** working in a bank... but that's another story. Let's get back to the dog otherwise she will really get angry.
"Today I only worked half a day, so I came home early," she says, "and when I came back Arthur was gone. Do you understand? He's not here anymore!" "Please don't cry! I understand, it's very clear, okay. **If you got back early**, how come you called me only an hour ago?" "Because I've been looking for him till now, I've looked everywhere. I thought my neighbors had taken him, they're so **envious**."
"Envious of Arthur?!" "Yes, why? You think you can't be jealous of a dog?! He is so special, he's such a great dog and you know he's part of the family. They are envious because they'd like to have a dog like him instead of having two **mangy** cats."

"Well, I didn't know there was a competition here for the most beautiful pet in town. Anyway, **let's get to the point**. So you've already tried to ask them, haven't you?" "They said they hadn't seen anything, they went to work early too. But their elderly mother lives with them and she stays in the house all day, she always **spies on** everything and everyone from the balcony, I'm sure she must have seen something, but she didn't say anything, not a word." "Maybe because she can't speak English? They're Mexican! Let me try to talk to her. Have you told Andy?"
"Yes, he said he'll be back as soon as he can, on the first available flight, he's as worried as I am." Well, I had hoped for something better for my first investigation, but I'll have to take what I can get, so let's start with the missing dog.

2 First of all, I decide to go and interview the neighbors. I knock, a **chubby** middle-aged Mexican lady opens the door, she is wearing a sombrero, which seems a bit **out of place** to me... until I go into the living room and I realize they're having a theme party, with loud Mexican music, tacos, tortillas and tequila. "Please, señor, eat something with us!" "No, thank you very much, I'm here just to ask some questions about my sister's dog, Arthur." "Again?! I've already said to your sister that we know nothing! Está loca! We have nothing to do with the missing dog. We don't like dogs, come and look at our beautiful cats!" she **holds up** her two beautiful Siamese cats, **which are far from mangy!** I start doubting my sister, like any good detective would. "All right, your cats are beautiful. Can I have a word with your mom? I know she's usually at home all day, she might have heard or seen something."
"I said we did not see anything." "If you let me talk to your mom, I'll bring Mr Burrito here tonight, he can cook burritos like nobody else." I win her over easily with that, promising burritos for todos. Here she comes, the old mother slowly getting closer in her wheelchair. "Good evening **Ma'am**, I'm sorry to bother you, I just wanted to ask if you have seen or heard anything by chance that might help us find Arthur, my sister's dog." The old lady (very old, she has to be more or less 120 years old!), with **wrinkles** even on her nose, is looking at me now. She gives me **a stern gaze** and from her **bewhiskered** mouth she says: "A veces, el rompecabezas no

es un enigma si no una trampa. A menudo no somos capaces de ver allí donde se encuentra la respuesta, justo delante de la nariz". "I'm sorry I don't understand Spanish, what did she say?", addressing her daughter who translates for me: "Sometimes the mystery is not a mystery but it is a trap. One often can't see where the right answer is, even when right under his nose."
"Uh. Well, very clear, I guess. So you...", but before I could finish the sentence, the old lady stops me with a gesture, as if to say "the oracle has spoken, it's your business now" and both mom and daughter go back to the party. **I'm about to leave** when I feel a hand on my shoulder: "Do not forget Mr Burrito! Now we are expecting him!" Of course, **my sailor's promise**... "Hi Philip, please, it's an emergency, you absolutely have to do me this favor, it's very important...", at least my Egyptian baker friend won't be bored tonight, I obviously got him a super recipe for burritos and a sombrero quickly bought from the second-hand shop nearby. Egyptian and Spanish are similar after all, aren't they? Okay, tequila will help. However, the situation starts worrying me, what happened to Arthur?

3 I decide to walk through the park where Linda usually takes Arthur, I keep thinking about the words the old lady with the mustache said... but what did she mean? I keep walking, I keep thinking, then I sit, I look at the colorful sunset and I think that tomorrow, Arthur or not, I'll have to go back to work, my real job.
So I decide to go back to my sister's house, with no answers. While I'm walking though, I notice something, a **leash** that says "Arthur" on it, it's near the park **fence**. **I pick it up** and examine it, **it's a clue** but I still don't know where it will lead me.
"Linda, I found this in the park, near the fence, how is it possible?"
"Oh my dear Arthur! I don't know how that happened, I don't understand, the last time he went out was with me last night, as I told you, and I had both his collar and leash with me, of course". She then opens a closet... an entire **walk-in-closet** for the dog's stuff, it's amazing and everything is also so **neat** and tidy, it even smells nice! If only my closets were like this, I think, what a waste of time and effort, just for a dog... of course these are just my thoughts and I make sure I lock them in my mind instead of **spitting them out loud**, as I often do.

"Here", she pulls the collar out of the closet but she can't find the leash. My ideas are developing but they still don't know exactly what direction to take, I start asking questions, a bit randomly:
"Do you have any enemies? Perhaps someone involved in illegal dog racing? Someone who wants to hurt you? Someone who could sell the dog? He's a **purebred**, after all."
"Well, I would exclude racing, he's a chihuahua." Ah yes, she's right, not really an option. "Someone who wants him for a show? A dog competition?" I say it as if I had found the solution to everything. "It could be! Yes, a dog show... there is a big one coming up soon and our Indian friends wanted to borrow Arthur and take him there, now that I come to think of it..."
"Well, call them immediately, think of a good excuse to meet up now, we need to talk to them." Linda hastily dials their number: "Hello, this is Linda," her voice is shaking a little, "I need to see you, my brother needs a new fireplace and would like to ask Albert for some advice." She ends the call, smiles and says to me "Bob, they've said they can see us in an hour."
"OK Linda, but I don't have a fireplace, I live in **a studio apartment** on the seventh floor of an old building!" "I know, it doesn't matter, make something up, you have always been good at improvising. Albert buys and sells fireplaces, he's very **chatty**, don't worry, you just have to **give it a go**."
Am I good at improvising? I didn't know that, I take it as a compliment, but I'm not convinced. We have to wait for an hour, a short amount of time when you have so much to do, but endless when you are waiting for it to pass...
"Do you want a coffee?" "Actually, I'd like a salami sandwich with fries, but if you only have coffee, I'll take it, or I can always **pop** next door and ask for a burrito." "Not funny. I can make you one of my maxi toasts if you want", my sister's maxi toasts are famous, but for all the wrong reasons. She fills them with smelly cheese and they are impossible to digest, but we are too **chicken** to tell her. "No, thank you Linda, I'm happy with the coffee, I don't want **to fill myself up**, we must be awake and **clear-headed** tonight."

4 Five minutes later the doorbell rings, it's Andy, just back from Paris, at least so I thought. The strange thing that immediately **leaps out** is that my sister and her husband seem cold and dis-

tant, not warm and loving as always. They have always been the model couple, who everybody admired, eternally in love. After a moment of embarrassment, Andy **blurts out**: "Linda, I missed you so much...", but he's only been gone a few hours, I thought. "Andy, me too! And in this terrible situation I've realized how much I need you, I'm sorry, I didn't really want you to leave, please let's find Arthur and go back to our life together." But what are they talking about?! I guess there was a **marital breakdown** and I knew nothing about it, that trip to Paris was just a cover, they had actually decided to give themselves a break. I speak: "Well well well, **don't air your dirty laundry in public**, I don't want to know anything, don't say anything to me, let's just go find Arthur!"

5 We go to their friends' house, my sister and Andy are **lovebirds** now, they kiss and hug. I feel a slight sense of disgust, but I continue to feed my ideas.
We arrive at Albert and his wife's home, they're very welcoming, very friendly and nice. They tell us they really know nothing about the dog, yes, they asked if they could take Arthur to the show but they gave up in the end, they were very sorry and blah blah blah. Albert also asks me about the fireplace, I try to make something up, when suddenly I hear barking. "Excuse me, what's this noise? It seems like a dog." "It must be our neighbors', he often barks, he's a good guard dog." "Hmm... maybe I should take a look." So I start walking around the house, but I can't see or hear anything. But I can smell something! A wet dog, unmistakable. It's coming from below, from the **basement**, I start slowly going down the stairs and... "Arthur!" I scream. The scene before me is far too sweet to be a **kidnapping**. Albert's little daughter, **a six-year-old girl**, is bathing Arthur, brushing him like a puppet, **cuddling** him. Suddenly, Andy comes **running up** behind me, he comes close and whispers in my ear, "I'll explain everything to you later, don't say a word, please." Back to the living room, Andy starts screaming with an angry and shocked tone "Albert, I would never have expected this from you, you really disappoint me. Linda, my love, let's take our puppy and go home." I hear Albert mumbling "But Andy, I ..." "Enough, don't say anything, I'll deal with you later."

6 The three of us return to their house, sorry, I mean the four of us, let's not forget Arthur. There is a heavy silence in the car, nobody says anything. I try to **break the ice**: "Well, **all's well that ends well!**" but no reply.

Back home, Linda puts the dog to bed, as if it were actually a baby, then with her head down she turns to Andy "It was you, wasn't it?" "What do you mean, love?"

"You wanted him to take part in that stupid show, you wanted him to win." "How can you say something like that, Linda? I would never do that, you know!"

"It was you..." I start to be very confused but I decide to tell them what I think: "I think Andy has done everything for good reason. I think that this morning, after you went out, he took Arthur to the park to clear his head. I think that he then deliberately **took Arthur off** the leash and deliberately wanted to make you believe the story of the kidnapping. I think he called Albert and asked him to keep the dog at his house. But I also think that he didn't do all this for the show, oh no, my dear Linda, he did it for you. He knew it would be the only way to **make up** with you, to get you to love him again. Andy, admit it, there's nothing wrong with that, **the ends justify the means**."

"Andy, is it true?" "Yes, my love, it's true! I was afraid of losing you, and I knew that Arthur would get us back together."

And there she was, in the perfect final scene, with the two of them hugging each other, romantic music in the background... oh no, that's the Mexicans singing. First case solved, I would say I was good. "Guys, **I'm off**. I have to get up early tomorrow and I'm very tired." "Thanks for everything Bob, you're always so kind, you're the best brother in the world."

"Thanks Bob" says Andy, but **he looks away**... I go closer to his ear... "Andy, **you got away** with this one. I know that you wanted Arthur to go to that stupid show, but for some reason my sister loves you. To coin a relevant phrase, **you can't teach an old dog new tricks**, and so if you **step out of line** once more, you can be sure it will be your last time. Now go and be with my sister, and make sure she stays happy." Andy stares at me "It was just a dog show, and anyway, I do love your sister." See? I was right, all's well that ends well!

PRACTICE MAKES PERFECT

1. GOT IT? - Reading Comprehension

Answer the following questions.

1 • Who calls Bob on the phone when he's on the subway? Why?

2 • Why does Linda say that Bob is cynical?

3 • Does Bob like Andy, his brother-in-law?

4 • Where does Linda work? Is that what she really wanted to do?

5 • Where are Linda's neighbors from?

6 • Who does Bob talk to at first, in order to get some information about Arthur? Does he get the information he wants?

7 • Who does Bob call to help him with some food and why?

8 • What does Bob find in the park?

9 • What excuse does Linda make up in order to go and visit her Indian friends? Why?

10 • Who finds Arthur and where?

2. KEY WORDS - Vocabulary

Match the word with its definition.

1	stubborn	desperate, agitated
1	frantic	someone who never wants to change opinions, obstinate
1	whining	hugging, embracing
1	regretted	dirty, unclean
1	(to) report	to come or go quickly
1	to downplay	to say that someone is responsible for something
1	(to) blame	to minimize, not to give much importance to something
1	crowded	a place you keep your clothes that is big enough you can walk in it
1	avoided	something you use to control and lead a dog or another animal
1	paranoid	when you desire someone else's life/things
1	envious	a strict/severe look
1	mangy	an animal of pedigree
2	chubby	clean, tidy
2	wrinkles	something used to mark boarders, a barrier
2	a stern gaze	it describes a person suffering from paranoia
2	bewhiskered	felt sorrow and unhappy with something done
3	leash	stayed away from something
3	fence	lines or creases on your skin, they usually appear when you get old
3	walk-in-closet	stealing someone, usually as a hostage to get money
3	neat	quite fat, round and plump
3	purebred	having hairs around the mouth
3	a studio apartment	the part of a house that is underground
3	chatty	full of people
3	(to) pop	to tell the police
3	chicken (adj.)	someone who talks a lot, talkative
3	clear-headed	a one-room apartment
4	marital breakdown	a pair of lovers
5	lovebirds	scared, not brave, not courageous
5	basement	a period of crisis for a married couple
5	kidnapping	free from other worries or thoughts, calm
5	cuddling	complaining, making a long and sad sound

3. FIND THEM OUT! - Phrasal Verbs Crossword

There are a number of phrasal verbs used in the text. They can be found in the paragraphs indicated below. Find the phrasal verb, match the context with the crossword clue, then add the phrasal verbs (infinitive form) to complete the crossword.

Across

1. *To make something full* (3)
4. *To become quiet or relaxed after a period of agitation* (1)
5. *To get older* (1)
6. *To come closer to someone quickly* (5)
11. *To say something suddenly, without thinking* (4)
12. *To secretly observe* (1)
13. *To become friends again, to reconcile* (6)
15. *To remove* (6)

Down

2. *To quickly become obvious or noticed* (4)
3. *To do something but not get punished* (6)
7. *To take up with the hand* (3)
8. *To eventually become* (1)
9. *To present or show by lifting* (2)
10. *To look in another direction to avoid someone eyes* (6)
14. *To leave* (6)

4. LOST IN TRANSLATION?

Translate the following sentences using the vocabulary and the phrasal verbs above.

1 • Tim è corso di fretta verso Tom e ha detto: «Li ho spiati tutto il giorno, sono finiti a farsi le coccole sul divano».

2 • Tom sentiva di essere paranoico a pensare che i suoi genitori stessero avendo una crisi matrimoniale.

3 • Lei vive in un monolocale e ha un pastore tedesco di razza, io vivo in una villa con una taverna e un giardino e ho solo dei gatti malconci.

4 • Ha solo fatto un salto e ha salutato, non ha nemmeno tolto la giacca. Quasi non l'ho riconosciuto, è cresciuto così tanto, era paffutello e chiacchierone!

5 • La mia insegnante mi guarda sempre in modo severo, le sue rughe mi spaventano, devo solo provare a distogliere lo sguardo e calmarmi quando succede.

6 • «Non la farà franca! Ha rotto il suo vaso antico e ha dato la colpa a me, non so perché è così invidioso, una volta ha persino provato a denunciarmi!»
«Smettila di piagnucolare e smettila di urlare, questo posto è affollato, ti sentono tutti. È solo un uomo vecchio e testardo, non ti arrabbiare.»
«Devi sempre minimizzare le cose, non mi piace, me ne vado, ciao!»

A BIT MORE...

IDIOMS/SLANG & MORE

The following idioms and expressions are used in the text, learn their meanings and try the exercise that follows.

Where is it?	What is it?	What does it mean?
1	a nine-to-five job	espressione usata per intendere lavoro *full-time*, otto ore
1	comin'	spesso, anche nel linguaggio colloquiale scritto, con le parole che finiscono per -ING si omette la G finale, tanto non si pronuncia, giusto? Ricorda però che si tratta di un uso colloquiale, informale
1	out of breath	senza fiato, con affanno
1	what a pity	che peccato!
1	he always pokes fun at people	si prende sempre gioco della gente
1	who cares...?	a chi importa...?
1	if you got back early	ricorda che *get* ha molti significati e spesso sostituisce altri verbi, come in questo caso, in cui *got* = *came*
1	let's get to the point	arriviamo al punto
2	out of place	fuori luogo
2	ma'am	sta per *madam*, abbreviata *ma'am* e pronunciata *mem* (Ae) oppure *marm* (Be)
2	I'm about to leave	si usa la struttura *to be about to* + forma base del verbo quando si vuole intendere «stare per fare qualcosa», in questo caso «sto per andarmene»
2	sailor's promise	promessa di marinaio
3	it's a clue	*clue* = indizio, spesso si dice *I have no clue* o semplicemente *no clue* = non ne ho idea
3	spitting them out loud	sputarli fuori ad alta voce (riferito ai pensieri, in questo caso)

Where is it?	What is it?	What does it mean?
3	give it a go	provarci, dare una possibilità
4	don't air your dirty laundry in public	lava i panni sporchi in famiglia
6	(to) break the ice	rompere il ghiaccio
6	all's well that ends well!	tutto è bene quel che finisce bene!
6	the ends justify the means	il fine giustifica i mezzi
6	you can't teach an old dog new tricks	le abitudini acquisite nel tempo difficilmente si cambiano. Il lupo perde il pelo ma non il vizio, anche detto: *a leopard cannot change its spots*
6	step out of line	uscire fuori dalle righe, fare qualcosa di negativo

CULTURE SHOCK!
Ae vs Be - American English vs British English

Ae	Be	Meaning
subway	underground	metropolitana
closet	wardrobe/cupboard	armadio
cell phone	mobile phone	cellulare
neighbor	neighbour	vicino di casa
favor	favour	favore
mustache	moustache	baffi
colorful	colourful	pieno di colori
leash	lead	guinzaglio
apartment	flat	appartamento

FOCUS ON...

PRONUNCIATION

BISCUITS = *BISKIZ* (1)

La pronuncia del dittongo UI è decisamente interessante... in questo caso abbiamo visto un esempio in cui si pronuncia come una I. Ma nella parola **fruit**? Oppure in **juice**? **Suit**? **Suite**? **Cruise**? Dunque...
Fruit = *fruut* = frutta, *juice* = *juus* = succo, *suit* = *suut* = tanti significati! Come nome di solito si riferisce al completo elegante da uomo o al tailleur per la donna, ma può voler dire anche «querela, causa legale». Come verbo significa «adattare, star bene», riferito a un capo di abbigliamento, per esempio: *this shirt really suits you* = questa camicia ti dona davvero/ti sta bene addosso.
Se invece parliamo della *suite* di un hotel, la pronuncia sarà *suit* , perché la parola deriva dal francese.
Cruise = *cruuz* = crociera (oppure il cognome del famoso Tom!).

Esistono vocali brevi e vocali lunghe nella fonetica inglese: il simbolo fonetico per capire se la vocale è lunga è formato da due punti dopo la vocale. Per esempio, nel dizionario troverai *fruit* = /fru:t/, con la "u" lunga. Perché è così importante? Beh, perché in alcuni casi cambia nettamente il significato di una parola a seconda che la vocale sia pronunciata breve o lunga.

Esempi:
this (= questo/a), vocale breve – *these* (= questi/e), vocale lunga
ship (= nave), vocale breve – *sheep* (= pecora), vocale lunga
Non ti sembra che ci sia una grande differenza? Prova a dare un'occhiata a queste parole, allora:
sheet (= lenzuolo, foglio), vocale lunga – *shit* (= ... !!), vocale breve
beach (= spiaggia), vocale lunga – *bitch* (= ... !!), vocale breve
Got it?

IT TAKES ME FOREVER TO GET TO WORK (1)

Il verbo **take** ha molti usi ma uno di questi, molto comune, serve a esprimere il tempo, quanto ci si mette a fare qualcosa, di solito inteso in relazione alla distanza. *It takes me forever to get to work* = mi ci vuole una vita per arrivare al lavoro.

In questo senso si avvale della forma impersonale *it* + verbo *take* coniugato al tempo della frase.

Esempio:
How long did it take to drive to San Francisco?
Quanto tempo ci è voluto per guidare fino a San Francisco?

CONVENIENT (1)

Esistono tanti **false friends** in inglese, tante parole che sembrano avere lo stesso significato dell'italiano ma che in realtà ingannano. *Convenient* è una di quelle parole, infatti non vuol dire «conveniente» ma «comodo, utile, agevole».
Prendiamo l'**esempio** dal testo:
I always wonder why you don't take the subway, it's so much more convenient and relaxing. Mi chiedo sempre perché non prendi la metro, è tanto più comoda e rilassante.

«Conveniente» invece si può rendere con le parole *suitable*, *appropriate* oppure *cheap*, se si intende «economicamente vantaggioso, economico».
La parola *comfortable*, invece, vuol dire «comodo» nel senso di «confortevole» oppure quando ci si sente «a proprio agio».

This new couch is very comfortable.
Questo nuovo divano è molto comodo.

I feel comfortable when I'm with you.
Mi sento a mio agio quando sono con te.

... WHICH ARE FAR FROM MANGY! (2)

To be far from = essere ben lontano da
Esempio dal testo:
She holds up her two beautiful Siamese cats, which are far from mangy! Solleva i suoi due bei gatti siamesi, che sono ben lontani dall'essere malconci/spelacchiati!

A SIX-YEAR-OLD GIRL (5)

Perché *year* non ha la S? Eppure gli anni sono sei, dovrebbe essere plurale. Perché in questo caso ha funzione di aggettivo, come se dicessi una ragazza "seienne".

She's a beautiful eighteen-year-old girl, I wish I were her age!
È una bella ragazza diciottenne, magari avessi la sua età!

Questo tipo di aggettivo si rende sempre con i trattini, gli *hyphen*, e può essere usato anche con altri tipi di sostantivi, per **esempio**:
It was a fantastic honeymoon, we stayed in a five-star hotel!
È stata una luna di miele fantastica, siamo stati in un hotel cinque stelle!

E, come ben sapete, se ha funzione di aggettivo, resta invariato nel genere e nel numero perché tutti gli aggettivi in inglese sono neutri.

5. LOST IN TRANSLATION?

Translate the following sentences.

1 • È stata una gita di cinque giorni, che peccato che sia stata così breve, siamo tornati prima di quanto avremmo voluto.

2 • Veniamo al punto, Eve, non ti piace il tuo lavoro ma ci metti solo dieci minuti ad arrivare lì quindi lo trovi comodo, per questo non vuoi smettere.

3 • Non fare promesse da marinaio, smettila di prenderti gioco della gente e trova una brava ragazza da sposare!

4 • Siamo arrivati in ritardo, ci abbiamo messo tantissimo per arrivare dai miei futuri suoceri, giusto il tempo di rompere il ghiaccio e siamo dovuti ripartire.

5 • «Perché Luis non studia inglese?»
«Non ne ho idea, forse perché non gli piace il suo insegnante.»

6 • Che importa se non si sono sposati? Hanno avuto un figlio, tutto è bene quel che finisce bene!

GRAMMAR TOPIC
REPORTED/INDIRECT SPEECH = DISCORSO INDIRETTO

They said they hadn't seen anything

Ci sarebbe molto da dire sul discorso indiretto, quindi cerchiamo di fare una sintesi che sia il più completa possibile.

Cosa succede quando passo dal discorso diretto
(quello tra virgolette, per essere concreti) al discorso indiretto?

Discorso diretto:
She asked: "What do you want?"
Lei chiese: «Cosa vuoi?».
Discorso indiretto:
She asked what I wanted. Lei mi chiese cosa volevo.

So far so good? Fin qui tutto chiaro? Bene, procediamo...
Un primo punto su cui soffermarsi è: quando si può omettere il *that*?

Esempio:
I think that you're right. Penso che tu abbia ragione.

Ma posso dire anche: *I think you're right*, senza *that*? In questo caso sì, anzi, suona molto più naturale. Vediamo quando si può evitare questo popolarissimo *that*.

• **Nel linguaggio informale**, dopo molti verbi usati nel discorso indiretto (*say*, *think*, *suggest* ecc.) ma deve essere presente in alcuni altri verbi, soprattutto intransitivi (*shout*, *reply*, *email* ecc.)

He said (that) he was going to London.
Lui disse che stava andando a Londra.
Ma *He shouted that she broke up with him.*
Ha detto gridando che lei lo ha lasciato.

• **Dopo gli aggettivi** (ma di solito non si omette dopo i sostantivi).
She is happy (that) you came to visit us.
Lei è felice che tu sia venuto a trovarci.
I agree with the fact that he wants to change job.
Sono d'accordo col fatto che voglia cambiare lavoro.

• **Nelle subordinate relative**, quando ha funzione di complemento oggetto (**non** di soggetto!)
These are the houses (that) we saw on TV.
Queste sono le case che abbiamo visto in TV.

Dopo aver chiarito questo argomento, torniamo a occuparci più direttamente del nostro discorso indiretto (scusa il gioco di parole)!

Ti sarà utile questa tabella, dove puoi trovare i tempi verbali corrispondenti da usare quando passi dal discorso diretto all'indiretto:

Direct Speech	Example	Indirect Speech	Example
WILL	the test will be difficult	WOULD	they said that the test would be difficult
PRESENT SIMPLE	he needs it	PAST SIMPLE	he said he needed it
PRESENT CONTINUOUS	he's driving very fast	PAST CONTINUOUS	he thought he was driving very fast
PRESENT PERFECT	it has been a fantastic trip	PAST PERFECT	he said it had been a fantastic trip
PAST SIMPLE	I played the piano with her father	PAST PERFECT	she knew I had played the piano with her father
CAN	he can cook very well	COULD	she thought he could cook very well
PAST PERFECT	I arrived late and I had missed my train	PAST PERFECT	he said he had arrived late and he had missed his train
QUESTIONS	where's Jordan? when are you going to Spain? what do you want to eat for dinner?	ANSWERS	I asked where Jordan was she asked when I was going to Spain he asked what I wanted to eat for dinner

Potremmo confonderti con altre regole o usi avanzati del discorso indiretto, ma per ora abbiamo detto abbastanza e hai tutti gli strumenti per farne un buon uso! *Let's practise...*

6. MAKE IT INDIRECT

Rewrite the following sentences using indirect speech

1 • "I can play the guitar." Betty said ....

2 • "We will stay in New York." They told us ....

3 • "They arrived a month ago." They told us..............................

4 • "I have never driven on the right." He admitted......................

5 • "I can't go to work." He said ....

6 • "Why don't you like the show?" She wondered......................

7 • "Where did you go?" He asked...

8 • "I'm just having a drink." Susan said ....

7. LOST IN TRANSLATION? MIX IT UP!

Translate the following text into English using some of the words and expressions you have discovered in this story:

«Non mi far pentire di averti raccontato i miei segreti.»
«Non preoccuparti, non sono una chiacchierona.» Jane disse che poteva fidarsi di lei. Jane prese le sue cose e se ne andò. Si chiedeva che tipo di segreti avesse confessato dopotutto, le aveva solo detto che ha una tresca con una sua collega, ma non è neanche sposato! La sua segretaria sì, ma è un dettaglio, o no? Comunque, "Che importa?", pensò, "Ho solo bisogno di tornare a casa e fare un pisolino". Tornò a casa, si tolse il cappotto e lo mise nella sua meravigliosa cabina armadio, tutte le sue amiche erano così invidiose della sua grande casa, così grande e così curata.
Il citofono suonò, era ancora Jack, lei aprì la porta d'ingresso e lui sparò: «Per favore, tieni la bocca chiusa!». Le sembrò un po' fuori luogo, replicò che aveva capito, non c'era bisogno di diventare paranoico. Lo salutò e andò direttamente a letto. "Se è così preoccupato di essere beccato, non dovrebbe sputare fuori ad alta voce i suoi pensieri come fa di solito!", pensò e poi si addormentò.

American English

My Fairy Tale

STORY 5

1 Once upon a time, or perhaps I should start like this: when I was little I wanted to do everything. You'll be wondering what everything means, I'll try to explain. I wanted to do every job, know everyone and see every country that existed in the world. People used to tell me I was an impatient, **restless** little girl who was never satisfied, but I was actually a happy person, very happy **indeed**. I had it all, a family that loved me, good friends and good marks at school, I took up ballet and I loved going jogging. But that was probably not enough for me, I always wanted more and more. Then I grew up, I learned to accept **my everyday life**, my routine, the good things that happened to me, I learned to accept that I could not do everything, I could not meet all the people in the world! We only have one life and, though it may last a long time, it won't ever be enough to do everything I really want, but **the best was yet to come**. I was **a jack of all trades and master of none**, and now I smile **whenever** I think about how young I was, how young my ambitions were. But there was still something, an empty space inside of me, something **missing**, or maybe it was someone.

2 Until one day, at the office, I met him, I met Ryan. It was not love at first sight but my **gut** knew he was a nice guy. I have always been **outgoing**, resourceful, cheerful, lively, someone who **befriends** everyone. He was always so **introverted**, reserved, perhaps too shy. So I wouldn't have expected anything from someone like him... I still didn't know he was a man full of surprises! One evening, as was often the case, I finished work late, **I was pooped**, I approached the elevator and I met him. We exchanged **a quick glance**, I smiled, not really **on purpose**, it just came to

me naturally. Maybe because I looked tired, perhaps because he was trying **to chat me up**, he asked me a simple "**How are you doing?**" and I simply replied "Tired, but fine, thank you. **How about you?** It's 9 pm and the only thing **waiting for** me at home is my fridge and it's empty! Do you know a 24-hour supermarket nearby?" Ryan: "Yes, there is one nearby, over there on the corner. What do you need?" Me: "Well, I would like to get some things for a salad for me and some food for my dog." We talked for a bit about diets and something healthy but fast to cook once back home, then we said goodbye. I kept thinking he was a **weirdo**, that we would never **get on**. The following evening I finished work late again, I didn't meet him. But that was the night he surprised me, for the first time. I was walking towards the car when I saw a shopping bag on it, and a note: "So you'll have dinner ready tonight and a happy dog. From a shy (but not **ordinary**) engineer...". I opened the bag and found some ready-to-cook food (the best brand in town) and a big bag of dog food. I started to laugh alone, it's always nice when someone thinks about you, especially if that thought also **turns out** to be useful! These unexpected moments **went on** for a few evenings, always a surprise on my car after work, but I never met or saw him, he also moved to another office so **we didn't bump into** each other anymore, not even at the elevator. I wanted to thank him, to tell him something, but I didn't have his phone number, and perhaps I didn't really want **to break the spell**. I really loved that strange courtship. One evening I found a great bottle of wine that was only half full, with one of his **unique** notes: "To a person who always sees the glass (and the bottle!) half full, enjoy it tonight, as you think about your favorite **wooer**. We'll drink the other half together, if you wish, sooner or later." Every time, after each surprise, I would laugh like crazy! Alone, in the parking lot, I would look around, holding his card **tightly** in my hands, hoping for a sign from him, maybe his eyes somewhere, looking at me, but I never saw him.

3 It was all wonderful but I was wondering how it was going to end. Until one evening I found a kind of map on my car, it was drawn by him, I remember that even his handwriting **struck** me, too

perfect to be that of a man! This map took me behind a small building where there was a park, and there was also a beautiful sunset that evening. I looked around, but nothing... quite disappointed I decided to go back when there he was, Ryan, right in front of me, with his deep dark eyes **staring** at me and smiling. We said nothing, we just started **to laugh out loud**! Then he took my hand and led me into his car: "It's cold outside" he said, even if I did not feel anything apart from the emotion of the moment, strong and sweet at the same time. It was all simply very romantic, natural, true. I was a **tough** girl, always have been, he had not yet won me over, but **he was surely on the right track**. This man had surprised me, I was **intrigued**, he had **suddenly** become attractive to my eyes. We sat in the car for hours, I didn't feel tired anymore, we talked about everything, he confessed his shyness, confessed he had been looking at me every night from a distance to see my reaction to his surprises. "I like it when you laugh, I like the idea that I can make you smile" he said, and **I loosened up**.
I began **to feel warm fuzzies**, but as proud as I was (and still am) I had to play the part of the insensitive woman for a while. We were saying goodbye when I said "Hey, when are you **gonna** ask for my phone number? I think **it's about time**, don't you?". He laughed and **nodded** "Of course, you're right! Sorry, let's do that immediately. I don't have any paper but I do have a pen, please write it here, on my arm". The batteries in both our cell phones were dead, but he always seemed to find a solution to everything.

4 We started **to hang out**, we talked a lot. It happened one evening, one of many in which we went out together, but it was the one that finally opened my heart. I was at home with my mom, I was chatting with her while I waited for Ryan:
Mom: "What's your favorite book?"
Me: "I've got many. Certainly one of my favorites is Ocean Sea, written by Baricco. Do you know it?"
Mom: "No, **what's it like**?" Me: "Beautiful. Special. Just amazing. Maybe because I love the sea but it is really nice, I love the way he describes things and people. It's not easy to understand **right**

away but it is very deep, like the ocean, in fact. There's a chapter I remember most of all, the part where one of the characters, Bartleboom, talks about his ideal love... very romantic. A man like that would be great to meet! Well, I'm off, Mom, bye!"
Mom: "Bye, have fun, don't be late." Oh, I remember that night... Ryan picked me up to go **downtown**. We actually went to the **mall**. Target: bookshop. I had to get some presents and I wanted to lose myself in print, as always. I could spend hours in bookstores, sometimes I still do, and I never get tired of it. I also like the smell of new pages, the **huge** amount of words on paper written by so different people, with the same goal: to communicate, to get closer to people. I allow myself to be attracted by book titles, their covers, their authors, by the newly published books. I **leaf through** with interest. I imagine what my book will look like, the one I might publish one day. Maybe, it will remain **a childhood dream**. I keep looking, I walk past the shelves, I read some excerpts. Meanwhile, Ryan does the same, at least that's what I thought, but he was far from where I was, as if to respect that situation where there's the need for silence and concentration and a bit of time alone. There was still that sort of silent respect for the other person's interests, it's like that at the beginning of a relationship. Meanwhile, I decided what books to get, mission accomplished.

5 Time to go back to the car and ready to go to the theater together. **I dressed up**. I have never been a high-heel person, I always preferred **loose** clothing and comfortable shoes, but I made an exception for him, I was elegant but simple. I left my long hair loose on my shoulders, just as he liked it and I put on the new perfume, orange scented, the one I had recently bought. He was well dressed too, a great **outfit**, but with sports shoes so as not to look too formal. We had a front row seat at the theater. A good show even if it was strange and... in Russian! We couldn't understand anything, but it didn't matter. For a moment we both thought it would be nice to make love backstage or on that empty side balcony. But we left that idea to our imagination, and we held hands under the seats till the end of the show. Now and again he lightly touched my skin under my skirt, maybe **by ac-**

cident, maybe not. I felt excited, the old men next to us looked a bit shocked, we laughed. We used to laugh a lot!
Another special evening together. He took me back home and before getting out of the car he said:
"This is for you." "What?" I replied, happy the surprises **were not over yet**. It was a white envelope, a simple white envelope, as light as a plain white envelope, but I could see something inside, a folded sheet. I opened it. I read: *(...) He puts down the pen, folds the sheet of paper, and slips it inside an envelope. He stands up, takes from his trunk a mahogany box, lifts the lid, lets the letter fall inside, open and unaddressed. In the box are hundreds of identical envelopes, open and unaddressed. He is thirty-eight, Bartleboom. He thinks that somewhere in the world he will meet a woman who has always been his woman. Every now and again he regrets that destiny has been so stubbornly determined to make him wait with such indelicate tenacity, but with time he has learned to consider the matter with great serenity. Almost every day, for years now, he has taken pen in hand to write to her. He has no names or addresses to put on the envelopes: but he has a life to recount. And to whom, if not to her? He thinks that when they meet it will be wonderful to place the mahogany box full of letters on her lap and say to her "I was waiting for you".*
She will open the box and slowly, when she so desires, read the letters one by one. As she works her way back up the interminable thread of blue ink she will gather up the years — the days, the moments - that that man, before he ever met her, had already given to her. Or perhaps more simply, she will overturn the box and astonished at that comical snowstorm of letters, she will smile, saying to that man "You are mad". And she will love him forever.
I remained silent, **astonished** at the **torn** page in my hand as if it were a sign from God. He broke the silence: "I have never read the book but today I was walking around the bookshop, I opened it and I found this page **by chance**, and I liked it. It made me think of you". What could I say? How could I make him understand that perhaps coincidences really don't exist and that nothing happens by chance? I smiled. I kissed him, our first kiss.

I got out of the car with a fantastic emotion inside and a feeling I had never felt before. Have I found my **Mr Right**? And I will love him forever!

6 I'm about to get up, but she's still awake, she calls me: "Mom, so that's how you and dad met, isn't it?" "Yes, sweetheart, that's how we met. I hope you'll find someone who will love you the same way." **I tuck her in** and give her a kiss on the forehead. She's sixteen years old, she's not a little girl anymore, it's no longer time to tell her bedtime stories, but she experienced her first love related **heartache**. I want her to know that love exists, that there is a time for everything. Mine is a true story, a true fairy tale, my fairy tale.
My daughter stares at me, her eyes full of hope and wonder, she asks me: "How will I recognize the man of my life, mom?"
"Honey, you just will." But she insists "How? How did you?"
"Close your eyes and give me your hand" I say. She closes her eyes, I take her hand and I touch it with my fingers, then I ask: "What have I done?" "You have touched my hand with your fingers." "And how do you know?"
"I felt it." "That's right, **sweetie**. You will just 'feel' your true love. Sweet dreams now." She smiles at me, I smile back.
Before going to bed, I get a bottle of water and empty half of it, I put it on Ryan's bedside table with a note: "To the person who always makes me see the glass (and the bottle!) half full. Thank you. Your wife, forever".

PRACTICE MAKES PERFECT

1. GOT IT? - Reading Comprehension

Answer the following questions.

1 • Who is being told the story?

2 • What is Ryan's job?

3 • Where did the protagonists have their first chat? What did they talk about?

4 • What was Ryan's first surprise? Did she like it? What was her reaction to it?

5 • What is the protagonist's favorite part of the book Ocean Sea?

6 • What kind of show did they watch at the theater?

7 • What did Ryan give her after the theater? What was in it?

8 • Summarise the contents of the page that Ryan ripped out of the book Ocean Sea.

9 • Why is the protagonist telling her daughter this story?

10 • What does the protagonist do before going to bed and why?

2. KEY WORDS - Vocabulary

Look at the definitions below, can you find the word(s) in the text that matches with the given meaning?

Par.	Meaning	Word/Expression in the Text
1	unable to relax	
2	stomach	
2	friendly	
2	to make friends	
2	a shy person	
2	a quick look	
2	intentionally	
2	common, normal	
2	not typical, unusual, original	
2	a person that likes someone and tries to gain their love	
2	strongly	
3	impressed strongly	
3	to look at something/someone deeply	
3	strong, hard, stubborn	
3	to become curious and interested in something/someone	
3	to express approval by making a quick movement of the head	
4	the center of the city	
4	shopping center	
4	very big, large in size	
5	not tight, comfortable	
5	a set of clothes worn together	
5	unexpectedly	
5	very surprised	
5	removed, pulled apart	
5	unintentionally, accidentally	

3. FIND THEM OUT! - Phrasal Verbs Crossword

There are a number of phrasal verbs used in the text. They can be found in the paragraphs indicated below. Find the phrasal verb, match the context with the crossword clue, then add the phrasal verbs (infinitive form) to complete the crossword.

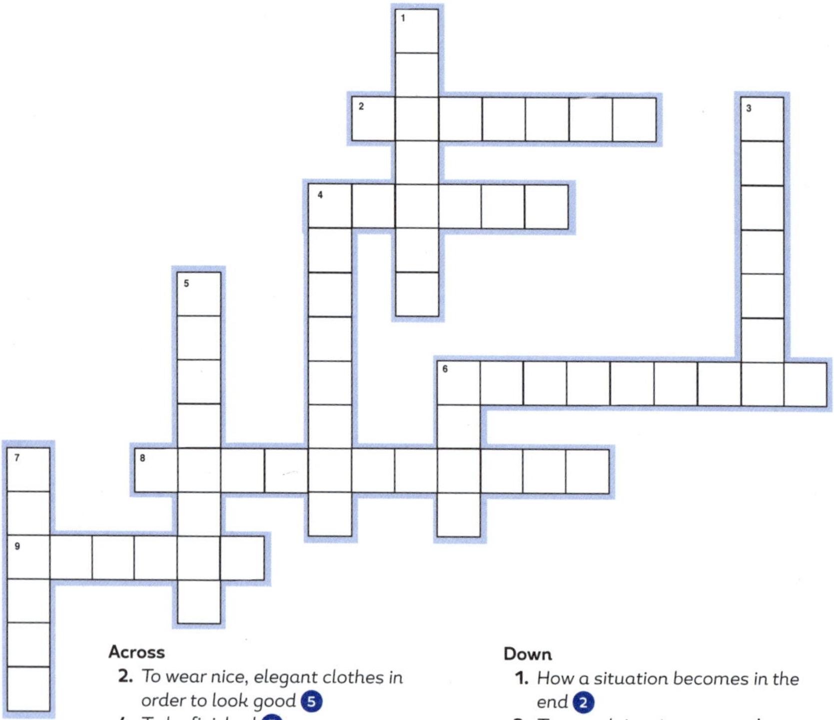

Across

2. *To wear nice, elegant clothes in order to look good* (5)
4. *To be finished* (5)
6. *To have a good relationship with someone* (2)
8. *To turn the pages of a book, for example* (4)
9. *To talk in a flirtatious way, with the intention of seducing someone* (2)

Down

1. *How a situation becomes in the end* (2)
3. *To spend time in someone's company* (4)
4. *To meet unexpectedly* (2)
5. *To relax, become less tense* (3)
6. *To continue* (2)
7. *To put someone to bed to go to sleep, for example a child* (6)

4. LOST IN TRANSLATION?

Translate the following sentences using the vocabulary and the phrasal verbs above.

1 • Stai attenta, non vuole diventare tuo amico, ci sta provando con te, mia cara!

2 • L'insegnante continuò a fissarmi e poi disse il mio nome e mi chiese di correggere i compiti.

3 • Sono andato al centro commerciale e ho incontrato per caso zio Tony, ha detto che verrà a trovarci presto.

4 • Avevamo l'abitudine di stare insieme così tanto, avevamo un rapporto così bello, non posso credere che sia finita.

5 • C'è solo una cosa di cui sono sicuro, non sei una persona comune! Ti vesti sempre elegante per andare al lavoro e sei un idraulico, ti sporchi ogni volta!

A BIT MORE...

IDIOMS/SLANG & MORE

The following idioms and expressions are used in the text, learn their meanings and try the exercise that follows.

Where is it?	What is it?	What does it mean?
1	indeed	una parola usata spesso per enfatizzare il concetto di «infatti, in realtà, davvero»
1	the best was yet to come	il meglio doveva ancora venire
1	a jack of all trades and master of none	*jack of all trades* = un tuttofare, *master of none* = specialista in niente. Una persona che sa fare un po' tutto, ha tante abilità ma non è davvero specializzato in qualcosa in particolare.
2	gut	letteralmente si riferisce alla parte dell'intestino/stomaco. Spesso usato nella sua forma plurale *guts*, in senso figurativo con il significato di «fegato, coraggio» oppure anche quando si vuol dire "segui il tuo istinto" (= *follow your gut*) o parlare di una sensazione di pancia, istintiva (= *gut feeling*)
2	I was pooped	slang americano *to be pooped* = *to be very tired*, essere sfinito
2	how are you doing?	un sinonimo colloquiale di *how are you?*
2	how about you?	*how about* è un'espressione che si usa nelle domande con il senso di «e che ne dici di...». In questo caso si intende «e tu, che mi dici di te?», ma potrei anche dire *how about eating out tonight?* = che ne dici se mangiamo fuori stasera? Se seguito da un verbo, come in quest'ultimo caso, il verbo in questione vuole la forma in -ing.

Where is it?	What is it?	What does it mean?
2	weirdo	un modo colloquiale per descrivere un tipo strano, strambo
2	to break the spell	rompere l'incantesimo
3	to laugh out loud	ridere di gusto. *Out loud* = ad alta voce
3	he was surely on the right track	*to be on the right track* = essere sulla strada giusta (letteralmente «sul binario giusto»)
3	to feel warm fuzzies	sentire le farfalle nello stomaco (come quando si è *in love*!)
3	gonna	slang che abbrevia: *going* + *to* = gonna. Lo stesso accade anche nel caso di *wanna* = *want* + *to*, per esempio
3	it's about time	sarebbe ora! O anche: finalmente!
4	right away	Subito, immediatamente
4	a childhood dream	un sogno nel cassetto
5	Mr Right	anche detto *Prince Charming* = il principe azzurro!
6	heartache	struggimento d'amore
6	sweetie	colloquiale, informale e figurativo per «amore, tesoro, caro, dolcezza». Letteralmente anche «caramella»

CULTURE SHOCK!
Ae vs Be - American English vs British English

Ae	Be	Meaning
elevator	lift	ascensore
favorite	favourite	preferito
parking lot	car park	parcheggio
downtown	city/town centre	centro città

FOCUS ON...
PRONUNCIATION
MY EVERYDAY LIFE (1)

Attenzione! Ricorda che: *everyday*, una parola sola, è aggettivo (= di tutti i giorni, quotidiano). *Every day*, due parole distinte, = tutti i giorni. Come nell'esempio del testo: *my everyday life* = la mia vita di tutti i giorni, ma *I go to work every day* = vado al lavoro tutti i giorni.

WHENEVER (1)

Eccoci ai cosiddetti relativi indefiniti composti con *ever*...
Ecco un riepilogo dei più comuni.

whoever = chiunque, non importa chi
whatever = qualunque cosa, non importa cosa
wherever = dovunque, non importa dove
whenever = ogni volta che, tutte le volte che, non importa quando
however = in qualunque modo, non importa come
Dall'esempio preso dal testo:
I smile whenever I think about how young I was...
Sorrido ogni volta che penso a quanto ero giovane...

Altri esempi:
You can come visit us whenever you want.
Puoi venirci a trovare quando (= ogni volta che) vuoi.
I'll accept whatever you decide. Accetterò qualsiasi cosa tu decida.

MISSING (1)

... there was still something, an empty space inside of me, something missing...
... c'era ancora qualcosa, uno spazio vuoto dentro di me, qualcosa che mancava...

Il verbo *to miss* vuol dire «mancare» in senso generico: tutti conosciamo I *miss you* = mi manchi. Ricorda però che significa anche «perdere», quando si parla di mezzi di trasporto: *I missed the bus yesterday* = ho perso l'autobus ieri. In questo caso **non** si usa il verbo *to lose* (= perdere in senso materiale). Se dicessi *I lost the bus yesterday* significherebbe che l'autobus è di mia proprietà e l'ho perso... forse qualcuno me l'ha rubato?

WAITING FOR + ASK FOR (2)

Un piccolo promemoria per un errore molto ricorrente.
Aspettare qualcosa o qualcuno = *to wait FOR something or someone.*
Dal testo:
... the only thing waiting for me at home is my fridge...
... l'unica cosa che mi aspetta a casa è il mio frigo...
Chiedere qualcosa = *ask FOR something*, ma chiedere a qualcuno = *ask someone*. Dal testo:
Hey, when are you gonna ask for my phone number?
Hey, quando hai intenzione di chiedere il mio numero di telefono?

WHAT'S IT LIKE? (4)

What is/are something like? significa «Com'è?» e si usa per chiedere il carattere di una persona o le caratteristiche di un oggetto. Nel testo, per esempio, ci si riferisce a un libro: *what's it like?* = com'è il libro? Me lo puoi descrivere? Se invece io ponessi la domanda così: **What do/does someone/something look like**? starei chiedendo la descrizione fisica di qualcuno o qualcosa!
"*I met Amy yesterday.*" «Ho incontrato Amy ieri.»
"*Really? What does she look like?*" «Davvero? E com'è?»
"*She's a very beautiful girl, long hair, green eyes...*" «È una ragazza molto bella, capelli lunghi, occhi verdi...»
"*And what is she like?*" «E che tipo è?»
"*She's a very nice person, she promised she'll help us with our English test*" «È una ragazza molto simpatica, ha promesso di aiutarci con il nostro test di inglese.»

AS vs LIKE?

La regola generale è:
like è preposizione, è seguita da un sostantivo o un aggettivo;
as è congiunzione, introduce un soggetto o un verbo ed è seguita da un'intera frase.
Jenny is a vegetarian like her mother.
Jenny è vegetariana come sua madre.
Nobody knows Nick as I do.
Nessuno conosce Nick come me (= come lo conosco io).
Nell'inglese parlato a volte si usa *like* al posto di *as*, con funzione di congiunzione.
ECCEZIONE: anche **as** può essere usato come preposizione (quindi davanti a un sostantivo o un pronome) quando si parla di ruoli lavorativi,

professioni ecc. In questo caso:
like = come, simile a, nello stesso modo di + sostantivo o pronome
as = come, in qualità di + sostantivo

Che differenza c'è? Proviamo con degli esempi:
She's speaking as a teacher.
Parla da insegnante, in qualità di insegnante (lo è)
She's speaking like a teacher. Parla come un'insegnante (ma non lo è).

GRAMMAR TOPIC: FUTURE PROGRESSIVE

You'll be wondering

Si costruisce con *will* + *be* + verbo in *-ing*. Ecco quando si usa.

A. Eventi futuri in progresso, in svolgimento. Qualcosa che accadrà in un particolare momento nel futuro.
This time tomorrow I'll be meeting my new boss.
Quest'ora domani incontrerò il mio nuovo capo.

B. Eventi che sono stati fissati o che ci si aspetta accadano. Non ha un uso propriamente progressivo in questo senso, si usa per esprimere qualcosa che è già deciso, che ci si aspetta che accada.
You'll be wondering what everything means, I'll try to explain.
Ti chiederai (= mi aspetto che tu ti stia chiedendo) cosa significa tutto ciò, proverò a spiegartelo.

C. Per esprimere qualcosa che dovrà accadere in ogni caso, a prescindere dalla scelta presente.
"*Do you want me to take you to the mall tomorrow?*"
«Vuoi che ti porti al centro commerciale domani?»
"*Don't worry, I don't want to bother you.*"
«Non preoccuparti, non voglio disturbarti.»
"*It's no problem,* ***I'll be going there anyway****.*"
«Nessun problema, **ci andrò comunque**.»

D. Esiste anche una forma di futuro progressivo con il *going to*:
I'm going to be working with Dave tomorrow, I won't come home for lunch.
Lavorerò con Dave domani, non tornerò a casa per pranzo.

5. LOST IN TRANSLATION?

Translate the following sentences using the "Focus on" and "Grammar" topics.

1 • Penserai che sono una tipa strana ma sento le farfalle nello stomaco ogni volta che vedo il mio cane! Sono così innamorata di lui, è il mio migliore amico.

2 • «Ho seguito il mio istinto e ho trovato il mio principe azzurro.» «Buon per te! Che tipo è?» «È così dolce ed educato.» «E com'è?» «È bellissimo, molto alto, capelli scuri, occhi azzurri!»

3 • A quest'ora domani sarò ad aspettarti in aeroporto, tesoro.

4 • Qualsiasi cosa tu mi abbia comprato, non posso chiedere di più, ho già tutto quello di cui ho bisogno. Che mi dici di te? Sei felice con ciò che hai?

5 • «Mi piacerebbe specializzarmi in qualcosa, ora sono solo un tuttofare e non riesco a trovare un lavoro.» «Sei sulla strada giusta, non preoccuparti, il meglio deve ancora venire.»

6. LOST IN TRANSLATION? MIX IT UP!

Rob: «Come stai?» Io: «Bene, che mi dici di te?» Rob: «Sono sfinito, è tutto il giorno che lavoro.» Io: «Era ora! Sei andato in Australia in vacanza il mese scorso, fortunato te.» Rob: «Lo so, mi sento rilassato ogni volta che ci penso. Negli ultimi giorni invece mi sento così agitato. Voglio cambiare lavoro.» Io: «Cosa?» Rob: «Penserai che sono pazzo, ma non lo sono. Ti ricordi Kris?» Io: «Sì!» Rob: «Beh, l'ho incontrata per caso ieri al centro commerciale e...» Io: «Com'è ora?» Rob: «È invecchiata, ma sempre simpatica. Ha detto che era stanca di aspettare il lavoro dei suoi sogni così lo ha creato!» Io: «Cosa fa?» Rob: «Prevede il futuro sfogliando libri. Qualsiasi cosa trovi nel libro è davvero connessa con la tua vita in qualche modo, ho provato!» Io: «Davvero? Allora è ancora una tipa stramba. Deve aver seguito il suo istinto, ricordo che lo faceva alle superiori!» Rob: «Anch'io ho un sogno nel cassetto... voglio lavorare in un orto, coltivare erbe e venderle» Io: «Ascolta Rob, so che sei stanco ma usciamo stasera! Per favore, torna a casa, vestiti bene e andiamo in quel lussuoso ristorante nuovo in centro. Ti prometto che il buon cibo ti farà stare meglio!» Rob mi stava fissando e io mi stavo preoccupando ma poi mi ha dato una pacca sulla spalla e abbiamo iniziato a ridere di gusto!

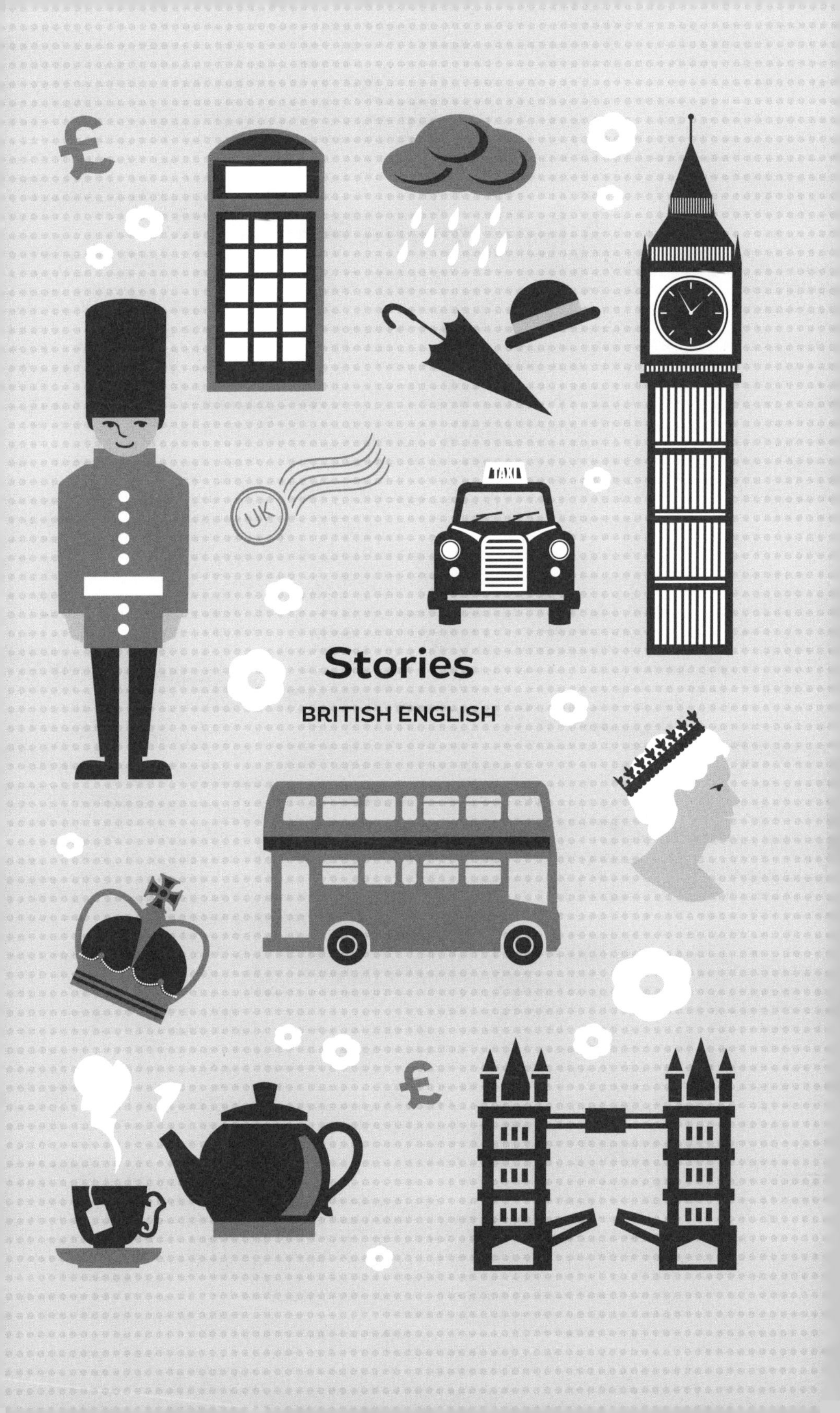

Stories

BRITISH ENGLISH

Be
British English

A Day at the Seaside

STORY 6

1 The day is **gorgeous**, he couldn't have chosen better. One thing he has learned from his adoptive country, Italy, where he's been living now for six years, is caring about the weather, and by now he has discovered all the most reliable weather sites on the Internet. For this reason he has been carefully checking the weather forecast for weeks, and he finally booked to go away with his family only when he was 100% sure no rain was due. None at all: zero millimeters of rain forecast with a 0% probability of rain. I mean, you cannot go wrong, can you?

He **never used to be** like that: rain, sun, clouds, **anything would do**. In Wales there was no need to consider the weather before going to the seaside, it was almost surely going to rain a bit! And it wouldn't have **mattered** anyway: the point is, the seawater temperature doesn't change when it rains, does it? So what's the point in worrying? He and his brother used to jump in the sea in any weather, like all the other children and parents on the beach, and **splash around** for hours, **to get out** only when it was time to go home, **shivering** and cold but so, so happy!

In Italy things are different, the weather is nicer, the temperature warmer, children can spend all day in the sea without going blue or getting frostbite.

2 He can't wait to spend the day on the beach with his children, it's the first time they've managed to organise something like this since the kids were born, five and three years ago: the idea of **queuing** for hours in the car with babies on board had always **put him off** the idea of travelling to the seaside for the weekend... and all their holidays have always had to be in Wales, where his wife **wasn't that keen on** going in the sea. She found it too cold

to walk around without a coat on, she would never have been able to get into the sea at those temperatures! She wouldn't allow the children to go in either. They are still little after all, she used to say.
Since he was a child, seaside life to him had always meant staying in a small caravan with his grandpa and grandma, listening to the rain on the roof. Of course it didn't always rain... but strangely this is what he remembers the most.
So, everybody in the car and off we go! Luckily the journey is only three hours long, because with the stops and delays for (in this order) getting the ticket for the motorway, getting petrol, going to the toilet, going to the toilet (no, not the same time), paying for the motorway, it took nearly five hours.

3 Finally there! For the first time in his life he can see the Italian Riviera, the place where the sun always shines (yes, ok, it does rain sometimes, quite substantially actually... every autumn there is news of new floods and disasters... but, looking at it now, it seems impossible!) and where all the Northern Italians go on holiday. **He looks around** for a bit... where is the car park? The roads are **packed with** cars, it must be true, the whole of Northern Italy must have checked the same website and they are all here for the weekend. That's fine, he **doesn't mind** walking a bit. Yeah, one kilometre is fine, it's actually a bit hard with all the toys, the beach chairs, the towels, the cold box and the umbrella, but it's going **to be worth it**! There is the seafront! But where is the beach? Why is it already completely full of umbrellas, that all look the same, and why are there all those little huts?
No, he's never seen it before, at least not like this... Ok, it's fine, the only question he's asking himself now is if they will be able to access the beach somehow. With all the stuff he has carried this far in 35°C, is he ever going to use them? The children are already complaining about the heat and he wouldn't mind jumping in the sea himself... "For goodness sake, let's just get on there and sit under one of those umbrellas!"
He's quite glad to be sat in the sun, if only the shore wasn't hidden by another four rows of tightly packed families with all their beach equipment and towels and bags, it would be perfect. Also,

the conversations from his "sun shade neighbours" are starting **to get on his nerves**. Who cares about what happened in that silly reality show last week, there is a reason why some people don't watch it (and are proud not to)!

4 "Ok kids, time for a swim, I'll race you to the water! ...more a gymkhana between deck chairs, but it'll be fine" he ventures. "Noooooooooooo!" A scream of horror comes from his wife. "Don't tell me she lost her **purse** on the way here, someone **must have taken** it while we were carrying all the stuff" is his first thought.
"They can't go in the sea yet, they've just eaten!" is the explanation. "Just eaten? But they only had a few biscuits in the car, and it was over an hour ago" "Yes, exactly, this is why they have to wait another hour, they could get ill, you don't want them to get cold and get congestion, do you?" "Cold? The sea cannot be less than 20 °C, and anyway, what's congestion?!?" "You never know, **better to be safe than sorry**! They can **dig** a hole here, while they wait for the danger to pass", she mumbles, while taking out all sorts of beach toys. "Oh well, at least the toys will get used", he sighs, thinking of the fact that he'll have to carry them back to the car with all the rest of the unused equipment, only this time it'll be uphill!
"But mummy, there's no space here!" the three-year-old complains, desperately trying to find some room between the umbrellas, bags, sun beds and chairs. Look, that area there will do (literally less than two square meters). The construction operation begins, supervised by engineer daddy who's in charge of getting the water from the sea (no, they cannot get wet, not even their feet). The complaints start "That lady keeps putting her feet on my sand castle". "The child next to us won't leave my mountain alone!" After another half an hour of **keeping the children away** from the water, and a hole big enough to swallow the old lady who was heading back to row 2, umbrella 26, the children are finally allowed to go near the sea. "It would be better if they didn't go in just yet, just let them play near the **edge**", says the mother, but surely he isn't going to stop them after all the time they've waited (and considering his childhood of swimming in 15 °C seas just after eating a memorable fried breakfast).

One of his thoughts, before following the kids into the water, is that they should reserve a part of the beach for non-smokers, because if he wanted to smoke he would just go and buy his own cigarettes, rather than smoke the ones of all his "sun shade neighbours!" Definitely not pleasant for an allergic non-smoker like him… "Ah-choo!" oh, oh, not already! He'll be OK, although he'll probably have to stand on the **shore** for the rest of the day. Here people are busy doing other things: swimming, playing volleyball in the sea, chatting, screaming, diving (no, not only the children, unfortunately), playing badminton and many other sorts of games, even some that threaten your safety or shamelessly break into your personal space. Not that he'd ever had much personal space since moving to Italy, especially in situations like queues and on public transport, and, it seems, also on the beach. **He's used to** the warmth of Italian people, their friendly attitude and their easy-going manner, he quite likes it actually. It is all related: he's sure that living close together is what makes Italians "unaware" of personal space and **it doesn't bother him**. It took him some time to get used to it, but now it's just part of life. He actually believes this is a better way of living, being part of a community **and all that**.

5 The sea is packed with people trying to escape the unbelievable heat: a colourful wave of swimming costumes and inflatables… this is not exactly a private resort in the Caribbean but the children enjoy it anyway! He must admit that it's a pleasure to be able to go into the water without that shiver down the spine he used to feel in that cold sea back in Wales. That lady over there doesn't seem to **be of the same opinion**: she's slowly making her way into the deeper water, wetting one part of her body at the time: **shins**, knees, thighs… she hasn't managed to wet her swimming costume yet. From the way she's arranged her hair it seems like she's desperately trying to keep it dry. He doesn't know how people manage to do that, when he swims he splashes and turns in such a way that the water goes everywhere, even where it's not supposed to (in his mouth, up his nose, etc.). "Dad, look at my dive! Ready, steady…" "Wait, be caref…" "…goooooo!". Oh. His son, with the biggest wave that could possibly be created by such a small individual, has just managed to soak the

woman from head to toe. Even her hair is wet, she'd better dive in now! She doesn't look happy at all... time to apologise: "Scusi tanto, mio figlio non l'ha vista". "Really?! Have I just said my son didn't see her?" he's thinking, looking at the beach and at the sea, packed with hundreds of people that you can hardly avoid to notice. Ok, he decides to pretend not to notice her **fierce** face: **if looks could kill**... Armbands on, it's time for proper swimming. He must admit he's not the **bravest** of swimmers, but he can still handle two and a half metres of water, can't he? The children are certainly more **eager** than him to go into deep water, so off they go ahead of him and they nearly get **run over** by a pedalo. Ah, they're actually trying to climb onto it while it's moving, not a good idea!

6 While he tries to convince his children to undertake a less dangerous activity, he notices people pointing at the sea, commenting on something. He wonders what's going on, and a murmuring starts coming from the swimmers. He can't quite hear what's being said and he struggles to recognise the words: "...tromba d'aria...". "What did they say?" he asks himself. His Italian is good, but there are still many less common words that take him some time to process. "Hmm... tromba d'aria... air trumpet... what is it? Hmm... I've heard this before... No, it can't be... I thought it meant 'tornado', but there can't be a tornado here, now. The weather is too nice, no clouds, no rain... I must **be mistaken**". The commotion is rising, more people are talking about this "tromba d'aria" pointing somewhere towards the deep sea. He tries to follow their fingers and actually manages to see, far far away, the small but distinctive shape of a little tornado! "Oh, look how beautiful it is, I've never seen one befo..." He can't even finish his thought, he gets interrupted by someone running past him, **rudely** bumping into him, as if he was in the way. At this point the news has spread, the whole beach is looking at the tornado and people are starting to get quite frantic. Everybody seems to be abandoning the sea to run towards their umbrella, people are quickly collecting their **belongings** and running towards the entrance of the beach. Some are going into the small huts for protection, some are actually leaving, the lifeguard is running around closing all the umbrellas, folding all the chairs and

beds: everybody is getting ready for the catastrophe. He decides to turn around to check how close the tornado is now, he must have got distracted, judging by the reaction it must surely be just a matter of metres away... Oh, no, it isn't much closer at all... he can **hardly see it**... and he's sure it's getting smaller and smaller, losing its power. **He turns around** and sees his wife walking towards him, Wife: "Where's everybody gone? I went to the toilet and when **I came out** the beach was suddenly all empty!" Man: "Yeah, I know, **they've all run away**."
Wife: "Run away? Why?" Man: "There is a tornado out there."
Wife: "A tornado? Where, I can't see anything, are you sure?"
Man: "Yes, there was... it disappeared... much like the crowd..."
Wife: "That's good, **I wasn't looking forward to** going for a swim with all that mayhem, now the sea is all ours!"
Man: "That's true, we've got the whole beach to ourselves! Some peace and quiet at last!"

7 His wife and children are there in front of him, enjoying themselves diving, playing, digging holes in the sand, laughing their heads off. The sun is getting lower on the horizon and the temperature is more **bearable**: this ended up being a lovely day, fun for everyone and full of new experiences... not only for his children!

PRACTICE MAKES PERFECT

1. GOT IT? - Reading Comprehension

Answer the following questions.

1 • How long ago did the man move to Italy?

2 • What two things in particular does the man dislike about sitting near other people?

3 • The children nearly have an accident in the sea, what with?

4 • Why are the man and his children so desperate to go into the sea?

5 • What will make returning to the car particularly difficult?

6 • Which part of England is the man from? (be careful!)

7 • What is the man's clearest memory of his childhood holidays?

8 • When the family arrives at their destination, what can't they find?

9 • What do the children put on before going into the sea?

10 • Why did the mother miss the tornado?

2. IN OTHER WORDS

Try to reword the following expressions, finding a synonym(s).

1 He never used to be like that =

2 his wife wasn't that keen on going in the sea =

3 the sea is packed with people =

5 doesn't seem to be of the same opinion =

5 he's not the bravest of swimmers =

3. KEY WORDS - Vocabulary

Match the word with its definition.

1	gorgeous	useful and rewarding, despite the difficulty
1	to matter	to break up/remove earth with a machine or tool
1	to shiver	the land along the edge of the sea
2	to queue	to be wrong
3	to be worth it	aggressive
4	purse	the front part of the leg below the knee
4	to dig	the things you own
4	edge	beautiful
4	shore	enthusiastic
5	shins	to be important
5	fierce	impolitely
5	eager	stand in a line to wait for something (like in a supermarket)
6	to be mistaken	can be endured
6	rudely	a small container for money (like a wallet) typically for women
6	belongings	to shake due to being cold
7	bearable	the outside limit of an area or object

4. FIND THEM OUT! - Phrasal Verbs Crossword

There are a number of phrasal verbs used in the text. They can be found in the paragraphs indicated below. Find the phrasal verb, match the context with the crossword clue, then add the phrasal verbs (infinitive form) to complete the crossword.

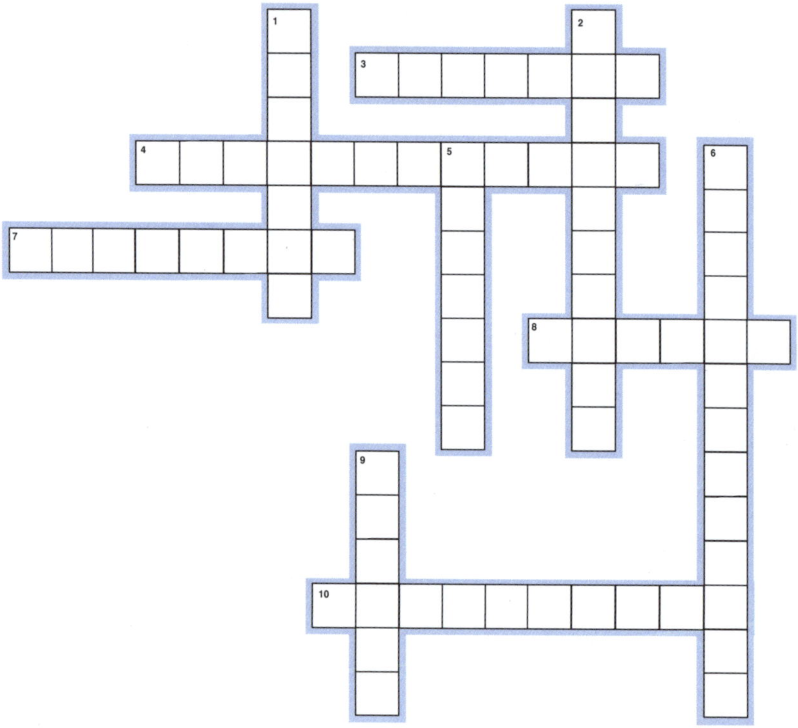

Across

3. To exit or leave a place (6)
4. To move about a lot in liquid (1)
7. To ensure someone remains distant from something (4)
8. To make someone not like or avoid something (2)
10. To study something visually (3)

Down

1. To escape (6)
2. To face the opposite direction (6)
5. To collide with something/someone (5)
6. To be excited that something is going to happen (6)
9. To exit from somewhere (1)

A BIT MORE...

IDIOMS/SLANG & MORE

The following idioms and expressions are used in the text, learn their meanings and try the exercise that follows.

Where is it?	What is it?	What does it mean?
1	anything would do/ anything will do	*what you have is sufficient, you don't need any more of something* («va bene tutto»)
3	not mind something	*it means you give general acceptance to something* («qualcosa non importa/ non dispiace a qualcuno»)
3	to get on someone's nerves	*to annoy or irritate someone* («dare sui nervi a qualcuno»)
4	better to be safe than sorry	*you should be cautious, otherwise you might regret it* («la prudenza non è mai troppa»)
4	something doesn't bother someone	*it means something isn't a problem for someone* («non essere infastidito da qualcosa»)
4	and all that	*everything connected with the mentioned subject* («e così via»)
5	if looks could kill	*used when someone uses a facial expression that indicates they are very unhappy with you* («se uno sguardo potesse uccidere»)

5. EXERCISE

Complete the following sentences using the idioms and expressions above.

1 • OK, he has an amazing body and a handsome face and..........., but his arrogant attitude just puts me off.

2 • I don't like to put too much money on my pre-paid credit card, I think it's ....

3 • "Would you like any more chips with your fish?"
"No, that....................., thanks."

4 • You should have seen the look on my wife's face when she saw me in the supermarket with another woman, if ....

5 • The dog next door never stops barking, it's really starting to ....

6 • His parents have always preferred his brother, but now that he doesn't live with them anymore it .... him.

7 • "I want to go to the bank before we leave town, is that OK?" "Yeah, I ...."

CULTURE SHOCK!
Ae vs Be - American English vs British English

Ae	Be	Meaning
caravan	trailer	roulotte
autumn	fall	autunno
kilometre	kilometer	chilometro
metre	meter	metro
biscuit	cookie	biscotto
apologise	apologize	scusarsi

6. EXTRA VOCAB – Parts of the body

*In paragraph **5**, the man speaks about the woman slowly entering the sea, body part by body part, "shins, knees, thighs". You are probably well aware of the common body parts: head, nose, arm, etc., but let's see if you know some of the more obscure body parts, we've given the first letter of each one to help you. If you don't know them, here's a chance to learn them!*

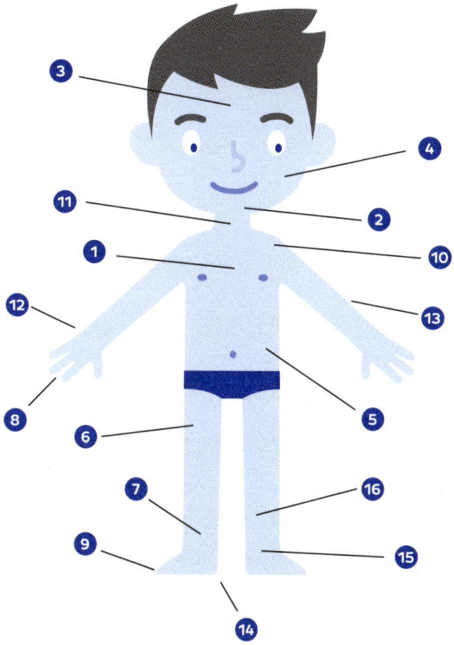

1 • petto: C. ....
2 • mento: C. ....
3 • fronte: F ....
4 • guancia: C ....
5 • vita: W. ....
6 • coscia: T. ....
7 • stinco: S ....
8 • dita delle mani: F. ....
9 • dita dei piedi: T ....
10 • spalla: S ....
11 • collo: N ....
12 • polso: W ....
13 • gomito: E ....
14 • tallone: H ....
15 • caviglia: A. ....
16 • polpaccio: C. ....

FOCUS ON...

TO BE USED TO (something or doing something) (4)

Indica che si è abituati a qualcosa (o a fare qualcosa) o che qualcosa non è più strano o problematico (ma è possibile che lo fosse in passato).

Esempi:
The hot Italian summers were difficult for me initially, but now I'm used to them. Le calde estati italiane per me erano difficili all'inizio, ma ora mi ci sono abituato.
I'm used to driving on the wrong side of the road now... there was a time when I thought I wouldn't get used to it.
Ora sono abituato a guidare sul lato sbagliato della strada... c'era un tempo in cui pensavo che non mi ci sarei mai abituato.
Nota: **to get used to (something or doing something)** è un'espressione collegata che descrive il processo di abituarsi a qualcosa .

HARDLY (6)

Hardly, in questo contesto, significa **almost not** = quasi non.
Vediamo qualche esempio.
I hardly know Peter, but he seems like a really nice guy.
Quasi non conosco Peter, ma sembra proprio un tipo simpatico.
I'll never pass the exam, I've done hardly any studying for it.
Non passerò mai l'esame, non ho studiato quasi niente.
What can we have for lunch? There's hardly any food in the fridge!
Cosa possiamo mangiare a pranzo? Quasi non c'è cibo in frigorifero!

Nota: dato che *hardly* ha già un significato negativo, non deve essere usato in frasi negative, altrimenti si creerebbe un doppio negativo (che in inglese diventa positivo!).

GRAMMAR TOPIC: MODAL VERBS IN THE PAST

(4) *Don't tell me she lost her purse on the way here, someone must have taken it while we were carrying all the stuff.*

Nella maggior parte dei casi, i verbi modali non hanno una forma passata: in questa frase si può vedere come usare i verbi modali per esprimere gradi di certezza rispetto a un evento passato. Usando **must have taken**, l'uomo si dichiara sicuro che qualcuno abbia rubato la borsa di sua moglie (in realtà non è così, ma questo è ciò di cui lui è convinto).

Questo modo di usare i verbi modali al passato è molto comune e importante da imparare. In questo caso, infatti, essi hanno usi leggermente diversi: vediamone i principali.

Gradi di certezza
Will + have + past participle = per esprimere certezza riguardo a qualcosa nel passato.
At the meeting they informed the employees about staff cuts, they won't have been happy about that. Alla riunione hanno informato i dipendenti dei tagli al personale, non ne saranno stati contenti.
Must + have + past participle = per esprimere apparente certezza riguardo a qualcosa nel passato (è una deduzione).
She must have lost her purse. Deve aver perso la sua borsa.
Might/May/Could + have + past participle = per esprimere possibilità riguardo a qualcosa nel passato.
They should be here by now, they might/may/could have got lost. Oramai dovrebbero essere qui, potrebbero essersi persi.

Impossibilità
Can't/Couldn't + have + past participle = per riferirsi a qualcosa che è/era logicamente impossibile.
They can't have finished the report already, they only started it on Monday. Non possono aver già finito il report, lo hanno iniziato solo lunedì.

Capacità
Could + have + past participle = per riferirsi a qualcosa che si aveva la capacità di fare, ma che non è stato fatto.
I could have gone to the match, but I decided to spend the afternoon with my children. Avrei potuto andare alla partita, ma ho deciso di passare il pomeriggio con i miei bambini.

Obbligo/Consiglio/Critica
Should + have + past participle = per parlare di un'azione passata che non è avvenuta, ma che sarebbe stata una buona idea.
"I have had this toothache for weeks." "Well, you should have gone to the dentist when it first started."

«Ho questo mal di denti da mesi.» «Beh, avresti dovuto andare dal dentista appena è cominciato.»
Could + have + past participle si usa per criticare qualcuno per non aver fatto qualcosa che si ritiene fosse sua responsabilità.
You could have helped me to prepare the presentation yesterday instead of just going home early, it's your client after all.
Ieri avresti potuto aiutarmi a preparare la presentazione invece di andartene a casa presto, dopotutto è un tuo cliente.

Third conditional
E non può certo mancare il famoso third conditional, che indica una situazione ipotetica nel passato (quindi è impossibile che accada), per cui tendiamo a usare **would...**

I would have gone to the pub if I had known a Rolling Stones tribute band was playing. Sarei andato al pub se avessi saputo che suonava una tribute band dei Rolling Stones.

7. LOST IN TRANSLATION?

Use the above focus topics to translate the following sentences.

1 • «Perché Elena non era alla festa?» «Non so, deve aver deciso di non andare.»

2 • Quando ero un bambino per me era un problema mangiare verdure, ma ora mi ci sono abituato.

3 • Non posso chiederle di vivere con me, non ci conosciamo quasi.

4 • Se me lo avessi chiesto, sarei andato con te al negozio.

5 • Non importa quanto io ci provi, non credo che mi abituerò mai all'accento scozzese.

6 • Quell'esame di fisica era così difficile, quasi non valeva la pena studiare.

7 • Vedo che hai comprato l'ultimo ZPhone, avresti dovuto comprare il Trident, è più economico e molto migliore.

8 • Avrei potuto aiutare mia moglie a lavare i piatti, ma ero così stanco.

9 • Questo pollo è quasi crudo! (*clue*: pensa a questa frase come se fosse «Questo pollo quasi non è cotto!»)

10 • Ho sempre lavorato part time, non sono abituato a lavorare fino a tardi.

USEFUL WORDS
conoscersi = *to know each other*
valere la pena = *to be worth + gerund*
lavare i piatti = *do the washing up*
fino a tardi = *long hours*

8. LOST IN TRANSLATION? MIX IT UP!

Translate the following text into English using some of the words and expressions you have discovered in this story.

Ad Adrian non importava non avere una ragazza, era abituato, perché nella sua vita, da quando era un adolescente, non aveva quasi avuto donne. Tuttavia era un ragazzo divertente, e così alle donne piaceva passare il loro tempo con lui; le faceva ridere a crepapelle con le sue battute. Un giorno, stava guidando la sua auto, quando fu distratto da un uomo con un grosso mento, si girò per guardarlo, non guardò dove stava andando e investì una donna che stava attraversando la strada. Uscì velocemente dall'auto per vedere se lei stava bene, vide lo sguardo sul suo viso, se uno sguardo potesse uccidere... Fu in quel momento che notò che lei era stupenda, aveva veramente una fronte bellissima. Adrian era impaziente di assicurarsi che lei stesse bene. Le chiese se stava bene e lei disse che le faceva male la coscia, ma che non importava, perché tanto aveva un'altra gamba. Adrian rise. Si stava rapidamente innamorando di lei, voleva invitarla fuori per un appuntamento, ma era preoccupato che lei non sarebbe stata veramente interessata a lui, ma decise di essere coraggioso e di chiedere comunque, e non poteva quasi crederci quando lei disse di sì! E ora, dieci anni dopo, sono sposati con due bambini e lui sa che se quel giorno non avesse investito quella donna, non avrebbe mai incontrato la ragazza dei suoi sogni.

USEFUL WORDS
battuta = *joke*
distratto = *distracted*
attraversare = *to cross*
appuntamento (galante) = *date*

Luc & Sarah

STORY 7

1 The alarm **went off**, like any other day, at 5.50 am. Sarah **turned over**, dropped her hand heavily onto the alarm clock and turned it off after the second ring. She never took long to wake up, and after two rings it was all unnecessary noise she couldn't stand, so early in the morning. She reached for her dressing gown, **slid her feet into** her slippers and got up. Every single movement was done on **autopilot**, with no time wasted: the **kettle** was ready to be boiled, the teabag was already in the cup, the milk waiting in the same spot in the fridge, the cereals and the cup were ready on the table, **the clothes had been chosen** the night before and left in the bathroom ready to be worn. She had breakfast and got ready to go out in **no more** than twenty minutes, she even had time to put a quick touch of **make up** on. She had perfected the technique over the years to allow herself to stay in bed as long as possible; when she wasn't late, and that rarely happened, she was even able to walk all the way to the station still half in dream world. She **grabbed** her bag and left her house. She couldn't hear a noise, it seemed like the whole world was still asleep.
Sarah got to the station, waited for the 6.32 am train, got on and, after exchanging a few words with the other **commuters**, **dived into** her book and spent the rest of the journey immersed in **another** world. When you need to get to the end of a book, even a one and a half hour journey is not long enough. The train called at her station, dragging her back to reality: the office and another day were just a twenty-minute walk away now. She just wished that something would happen to prove that she had made the right decisions in life.

2 "No, I can't believe it, I've done it again!" was Luc's first thought when he saw the time. It was ten to eight and he didn't know how

he had managed to **oversleep** three times in the last two weeks. "Good average!", he thought. Last night, after the match had finished so badly, dumping them out of the European Champions League once again, he decided to stay up to watch a ridiculous old film which he couldn't bring himself to turn off despite the complete lack of a plot. There was no excuse for being late again for work, he had to make a move. He threw the covers back – his entire life he had never seen the need to make the bed, you're just going to mess it up again later. Unless you have special plans... but it wasn't the case for him that night – and put on the first clothes he found in the cupboard "Yeah, blue shirt and orange tie, that'll do". There was no time for a cup of tea, he had to wait until he got to the office, could he survive that long? He grabbed an apple, his wallet, smartphone, keys, and computer bag. Ready to go. The gym bag was already in the **boot**, he **was supposed to go** last night, but he abandoned the idea and decided to postpone to tonight. Luc's office was only about thirty minutes away from home, and with **flexi-time** he only had to get there before 8.30. Quite early, compared to other companies, but, as a manager, he was **supposed to set the example**, so 8.30 it was. He just hoped the M25 wasn't going to be too busy this morning – was it ever going to be possible? – and saw the familiar warning "J18 – J15. Long delays". Wow, for once the traffic wasn't in his direction, so, in the record time of twenty-eight minutes, he got into the office building, went straight to his desk and made himself his first, deserved, cup of tea of the day. Done! Luc looked at his e-mails and at his diary. Things looked promising; apart from a chat with his boss – Luc wondered what he wanted to speak to him about – the rest of the day was just routine work.

3 "Good morning **Ms** Curtis, there's something for you!" Patricia was always very **sunny** and helpful to anybody who turned up at the reception desk, but Sarah felt that she was even more enthusiastic this morning. She didn't have time to finish her thought before Patricia handed her an enormous bunch of flowers "They arrived one hour ago, there is a card with them!". Completely astonished, Sarah managed to get into the lift with the flowers – yes, there were really that many – got to her desk, sat down and opened the card. "NOOOOO it can't be!!! That man from the HR

department **hasn't given up yet**!" After the box of chocolates for Valentine's day, the invite to go to the theatre for her birthday – which she **firmly turned down** – this was **the straw that broke the camel's back**. Considering how many times she had already confronted him and explained the situation, nothing seemed to work. Probably the worst part was the message "See you later in the canteen. Frank". Argh! "That means no lunch for me today!" she thought.

The smell of the flowers spread all over the office and, by 9 am, Sarah started hearing the first sneezes. By 11 am Helen's eyes **were watering** and she was all **blocked up**, as if she had the biggest cold ever. At 1 pm Helen could **hardly** breathe, all the windows had been opened and the flowers had been distributed to all the other teams, including HR. If Frank still had any doubts...

Helen recovered just enough to go for lunch and brought back from the canteen an apple and the description of a broken Frank. The rest of the day passed with no other major events, apart from Sarah trying to hide from Frank when he tried to ambush her a couple of times. When she saw a message from the girls, asking her to stop for a drink before going home, she accepted: Lucinda lived close to her and offered to give her a lift home. They all left the office together, escorting Sarah as if they were her bodyguards. Finally out, straight to the pub now!

4 Luc was still at his desk when he received an e-mail from Ed, who had found out that a new pub had recently opened, and was inviting some friends for a pint on the way home from work. Luc didn't really have to think too hard about it, the decision to join him was made in about 3.5 seconds. The gym was postponed, once again. After all, what are yearly subscriptions for?

The meeting with his boss was set for 1.30 pm. Luc knocked on the door, was invited in, sat down and after **exchanging a few pleasantries**, his boss **got straight to the point**.

Boss: "We are having problems closing that deal with FTR Consulting, their CEO is very unhappy with us and is making things difficult. They're insisting that we apologise and if we don't, the agreement might **fall through**."

Luc: "I've been dealing with it, everything has been fine! I don't understand what they are so upset about."

Boss: "The CEO didn't like your manners, too disrespectful apparently." Luc: "Are you serious? What did I do?"
Boss: "You called him by his first name and..."
Luc: "Him? What are you talking about? The CEO is a woman, her name's Kim Taylor. I would never have called her by her first name, Kim!"
Boss: "Exactly, you should have! He has Korean origins, his surname's Kim and he's a man!".
Luc froze, what had he done? Not just via e-mail, but also over the phone! During the conference call he had wondered how a woman could possibly sound so masculine, but he quickly dismissed the thought. He apologised to his boss and went to his office to make one of the most **awkward** phone calls of his life. Luckily, Kim Taylor took it well and now that everything was clarified he seemed ready to sign the contract. What a day. Luc drove to the pub still feeling silly for what he had done. Ok, time to relax now. Ed and Mark arrived at the same time and met him in the car park.

5 Nice pub, but what's the point of the incredibly loud music? The three men went to the bar, Ed paid for the first **round** and they went to sit at a table just around the corner, almost hidden. Luc's attention was immediately drawn to a group of girls; they were talking and laughing, trying to speak to each other over the loud music. They seemed to be having a good time. With her back to him, Sarah couldn't see Luc. How pretty she was, Luc thought, with her dark hair, **slim** figure and, when she turned to her side, he could see her deep brown eyes and her elegant profile. He considered going over to her table, but **decided against it**. Dan was more than half-an-hour late when he got to the pub, he walked around trying to find Luc and the others with a concerned expression on his face, and finally **spotted** them in the corner "Luc! You bad man, are you trying to hide from me?" he said with a laugh. Sarah heard him and turned around, curious to see who he was speaking to. She saw the boys greeting Dan, patting him on the back and shaking his hand. She kept her eyes on them until Luc saw her staring, he lifted his hand as if to say hello and gave her a broad smile. At that point she thought about getting up and going over there, but, after a long day without food, the waitress arriving with her dinner made her change her mind.

She had nearly finished eating when Luc approached the table "Hello, that looks nice, what is it?". "Hi, some sort of speciality of the house, I don't recommend it, the meat is dry," she replied. "Not a good start for a new pub. The beer is good though, at least they are doing something right." "I wouldn't know, I'm having a Gin & Tonic. You can't really go wrong with that." "You're right, if they managed to mess that up, they really would be in the wrong business!" The conversation was cut short by Sarah's phone ringing; she looked at the display and saw it was from work, HR department "Sorry, I need to take this," she got up and headed outside. Sarah was standing outside the door; she had a very intent expression and was clearly agitated by the conversation, but also seemed like someone who was not going **to give in**. Luc thought she was "sexy"; probably superficial, but, hey, that was the way he felt. While looking at her, Luc wondered if the right time had come, if it was the moment to take that step he'd always been afraid of taking. He looked at Sarah again and felt ready for it. But was it the right moment? Should he perhaps wait a bit longer? He wasn't someone who normally dived into things... No, it had already taken him long enough to get to this point, it felt right to do it, so he decided to try. Waiting could mean losing the chance forever. He sat there, looking at Sarah: at one point she looked in his direction, met his **gaze**, for a second got distracted from the phone call and smiled at him. His heart brightened up, making him feel even more ready.

6 When, 10 minutes later, Sarah **hung up**, Luc didn't wait for a second and walked in her direction. She wasn't looking at him, still engrossed in her phone. "Is everything ok?" he asked, nearly making her jump. "Yeah, everything's alright, just some issues at work... but let's not talk about it. Do you want another drink?" Frank had just promised to leave her alone, he had finally understood she wasn't interested, but this was an achievement she wasn't ready to share just yet. "I was wondering," Luc ventured "if you'd rather come home with me. It's much quieter there, easier to talk. I also put a good bottle of white wine in the fridge to chill last night, perhaps you'd like to share it with me?". Sarah stared at him. He wasn't a **strikingly** handsome man, but she found him attractive, he also **had a way about him** that she quite liked. He

was smiling reassuringly at her and in that moment she felt safe. It was definitely the right thing to do, go. Her friends were looking, they were whispering to each other, Lucinda gave her the thumbs-up as if to say goodbye, Sarah smiled and turned around to follow Luc.

7 They didn't exchange many words in the car, but they smiled at each other when Luc turned into the driveway and parked the car in front of the door. They got out and Luc lead the way, he put his hand in his pocket to get the keys. They weren't there. He tried the other pocket – they weren't there either – and he opened his computer bag, but the keys were nowhere to be seen. Panic! Where are they? They must be in there, he had them this morning, he could remember locking the door after..."You're always the same! Don't tell me you woke up late again and forgot to lock the door properly when you left!" Sarah had a teasing expression on her face, she took out her set of keys and opened the door. "But... I... maybe..." "Come on, let's go in, I'm tired and I can't wait to have a shower," she dropped the bag on the floor in the same place where she found it that morning, **kicked her shoes off** and let herself fall onto the sofa.

8 "This is the moment," thought Luc, reaching for his computer bag. He took out a small box he had bought the week before, which was safely hidden in there. He took Sarah's hand and started a **long rehearsed** speech which didn't exactly come out as he intended. It didn't matter, she had almost given up hope of ever hearing it, so she was happy to hear anything. She looked into Luc's eyes "I've dreamt about this since I was a little girl: back then I never imagined my Prince Charming would be colour blind!". "What? You know I'm not colour blind!" "Do you mean you intended to wear that tie with that shirt? That's even worse!" "What's wrong with my tie? I rather like it!" "The tie's fine, just not with that blue shirt!" "Are you sure? Perhaps this could be a way of keeping the other women away from me!" They both laughed.

9 Sarah wore the ring through the shower and some tidying up. That night they both got into their untidy bed, happy about the new adventure they had just started. Together.

PRACTICE MAKES PERFECT

1. GOT IT? - Reading Comprehension

Answer the following questions.

1 • What was the last thing Sarah did before leaving the house?

2 • What feeling did Sarah have when she left the house?

3 • While Sarah was walking to work, what did she desire?

4 • Why was Luc relieved when he saw the motorway information sign?

5 • Why was Luc happy after checking his e-mails and diary?

6 • Why did Sarah have difficulty getting into the lift?

7 • What surprised Luc during the conference call?

8 • What did Luc notice shortly after arriving at the pub?

9 • Why did Sarah decide not to go over to Luc's table?

10 • What was Luc's fake excuse for wearing the bad shirt/tie combination?

2. IN OTHER WORDS

Try to reword the following expressions, finding a synonym(s).

1 in no more than twenty minutes =

2 he was supposed to go last night =

3 Patricia was always very sunny and helpful =

3 Helen could hardly breathe =

8 and started a long rehearsed speech =

3. KEY WORDS - Vocabulary

Match the word with its definition.

1	autopilot	a person who travels a significant distance to get to work
1	kettle	in a strong way
1	make-up	difficult or embarrassing
1	to grab (sth)	a space in a car for carrying items
1	commuter	thin
2	to oversleep	a long look
2	boot	cosmetic products for enhancing the appearance
2	flexi-time	doing something without thinking about it
3	firmly	when breathing through the nose is difficult due a cold or allergy
3	to water	to see or notice someone/something
3	to be blocked up	to sleep longer than intended
4	awkward	to take something quickly
5	slim	in a way that attracts attention
5	to spot	a container for boiling water
5	gaze	when the eyes start to fill with water
6	strikingly	a system that enables employees to work flexible hours

4. FIND THEM OUT! - Phrasal Verbs Crossword

There are a number of phrasal verbs used in the text. They can be found in the paragraphs indicated below. Find the phrasal verb, match the context with the crossword clue, then add the phrasal verbs (infinitive form) to complete the crossword.

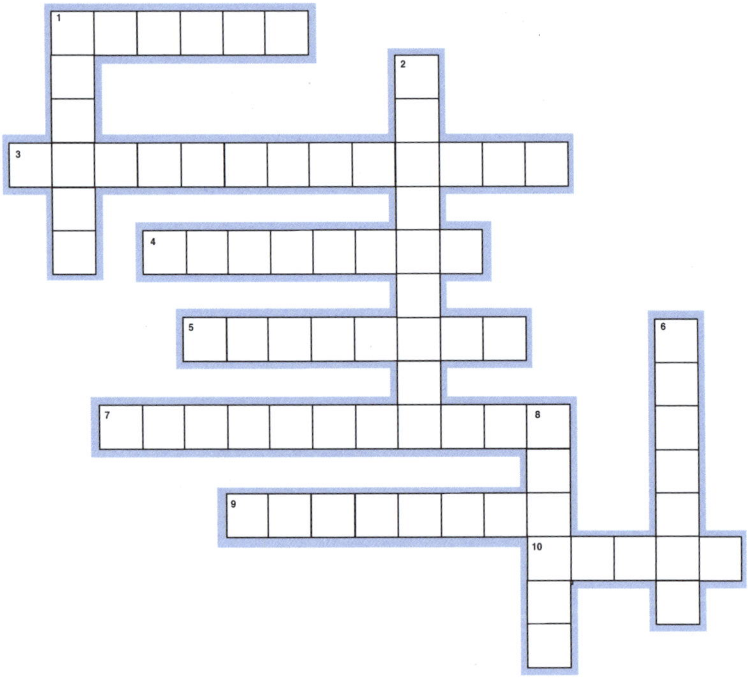

Across

1. *To quit doing something* 3
3. *To choose not to do something* 5
4. *To move your position by rolling from one side to the other* 1
5. *To start doing something with great enthusiasm* 1
7. *To fail* 4
9. *To reject something* 3
10. *To begin to sound (e.g. an alarm)* 1

Down

1. *To stop opposing something* 5
2. *To insert something into something else very easily* 1
6. *To flick something from the foot (e.g. a sock)* 7
8. *To end a telephone call* 6

A BIT MORE...

IDIOMS/SLANG & MORE

The following idioms and expressions are used in the text, learn their meanings.

Where is it?	What is it?	What does it mean?
2	to set an example	*to behave in a way that should be copied by other people* («dare il buon esempio»)
3	the straw that broke the camel's back	*when you reach the final limit, normally referring to patience* («la goccia che fa traboccare il vaso»)
4	to exchange pleasantries	*means to exchange a few polite words (e.g. greetings) when you meet someone* («scambiarsi i convenevoli»)
4	to get straight to the point	*to talk about the most important thing* («andare dritto al punto»)
5	a round	*is an alcoholic drink for each person in a group served at the same time* («un giro»)
6	someone has a way about them	*when someone has a certain charm or quality that makes them attractive but is difficult to define* («qualcuno ha un certo modo di fare/non so che»)

5. EXERCISE

Complete the following sentences using the idioms and expressions above.

1 • You are older than your sister, you should be.......... her an ......

2 • He's never had trouble getting women, he just ....that they seem to like.

3 • My brother has a reputation for being mean, indeed, he's always the last one to buy .... in the pub.

4 • Please, just ...., are you going to sack me or not?

5 • They introduced themselves and .... before starting the negotiation.

6 • I had put up with his complaining for years, but when he told me I was starting to look fat, I had to leave him, it was ....

CULTURE SHOCK!
Ae vs Be - American English vs British English

Ae	Be	Meaning
dressing gown	bathrobe	accappatoio
boot	trunk	baule
speciality	specialty	specialità

FOCUS ON...
ANOTHER (1)

La maggior parte degli studenti d'inglese pensano di saper usare correttamente *another*, ma in realtà parecchi errori sono causati dalla confusione che circonda questa parola. Tutti sanno che *another* è usato con sostantivi singolari numerabili...

Esempio:
I need another pint of beer. Ho bisogno di un'altra pinta di birra.

Spesso si crede che con sostantivi non numerabili, e in particolar modo con sostantivi plurali, si usi *other*, ma in realtà in inglese si usa **more**:
I need some more pints of beer.

Il problema si presenta quando sostantivi plurali sono usati in espressioni che contengono un numero o espressioni come *few/couple* ecc.: in questo caso si deve usare *another* e non *other*.

Esempi:
I've got another seven chapters to read before I finish this book.
Ho altri sette capitoli da leggere prima di finire questo libro.

My wife wanted another couple of children, but after we had the first one, I said: "No way". Mia moglie voleva un altro paio di figli, ma dopo che abbiamo avuto il primo ho detto: «Non se ne parla nemmeno».

SUPPOSED TO (2)

Supposed to, in questo contesto, significa *should*, per riferirsi a ciò che qualcuno deve fare (in base a leggi o regolamenti) o ciò che ci si aspetta che accada. Vediamo qualche esempio.

You are supposed to submit your expenses claim before the end of the month, if you don't, you probably won't be reimbursed.
Dovresti presentare i tuoi rimborsi spesa prima della fine del mese, se non lo fai, probabilmente non sarai rimborsato

The train was supposed to arrive at 9 am, but it didn't get here until after 10.
Il treno sarebbe dovuto arrivare alle 9, ma non è arrivato fino a dopo le 10.

Cats are supposed to hate water, but our neighbour's cat is always swimming in our pool. I gatti dovrebbero odiare l'acqua, ma il gatto del nostro vicino nuota sempre nella nostra piscina!

MS (3)

Ms è l'appellativo che viene automaticamente usato con il cognome (o con nome e cognome) di una donna; è un modo neutro di rivolgersi a una donna senza fare alcun riferimento al suo stato civile (sposata o nubile). È l'equivalente femminile di *Mr*; al giorno d'oggi molti credono che debba sempre essere usato, specialmente in ambito lavorativo, a meno che non si sappia per certo che una donna preferisca essere chiamata *Miss* o *Mrs*.

Good afternoon Ms Bowyer, how can I help you?
Buon pomeriggio signora Bowyer, come posso aiutarla?

Nota: la pronuncia di Ms è */miz/*.

GRAMMAR TOPIC:
PASSIVE TENSE

Una veloce revisione dei tempi passivi serve sempre, no?

1 *the clothes had been chosen the night before...*

Quello sopra è un perfetto esempio di *past perfect passive*. I tempi passivi sono formati introducendo l'ausiliare **to be** e usando il participio passato del verbo principale, la costruzione esatta dipende dal tempo verbale.

Tense	Active Voice	Passive Voice
Present simple	Elena irons the clothes	the clothes are ironed by Elena
Present continuous	George is making an apple pie	the apple pie is being made by George
Past simple	Shakespeare wrote *Macbeth*	*Macbeth* was written by Shakespeare
Past continuous	the decorators were painting the house	the house was being painted by the decorators
Present perfect	they have built a new hotel in our town	a new hotel has been built in our town
Past perfect	Sarah had chosen the clothes	the clothes had been chosen by Sarah
Simple future (will)	they will finish the project by the weekend	the project will be finished by the weekend

Le forme passive si usano per accentrare l'attenzione sulla cosa che subisce l'azione, che diventa la parte più importante (e quindi il soggetto) della frase. La persona (o la cosa) che compie l'azione può essere o meno inclusa, preceduta da *by*, nella parte finale della frase.

È anche possibile usare la forma passiva quando non si sa chi compie l'azione o quando non lo si vuole dire (ad esempio per essere cortesi e non incolpare nessuno: *the computer has been broken* invece di *Mike has broken the computer*).

6. BE PASSIVE - Exercise

The passive form has been used on a number of occasions in the story (paragraphs numbers given below): find the sentence and write it.

Example: (1) the clothes had been chosen

((1); (3); (3); (4); (4); (4); (5); (5))

7. LOST IN TRANSLATION?

Translate the following sentences.

1 • La scorsa settimana la chitarra di John Lennon è stata venduta all'asta, è stata comprata da un collezionista anonimo.

2 • Quando contatti il reparto vendite devi parlare o con il signor Taylor o con la signora Walker.

3 • Ho già perso cinque chili, ma per raggiungere il mio obiettivo ne devo perdere altri undici.

4 • Oggi Paul avrebbe dovuto spedire la relazione di fine mese al CEO, ma è già andato a casa, deve essersi dimenticato.

5 • L'auto verrà riparata prima che ritorni la signora Dean?

6 • Dobbiamo trovare altre £10.000, altrimenti non saremo in grado di comprare la nostra casa dei sogni.

7 • Quando diventi residente in uno stato estero, dovresti pagare le tasse in quello stato.

8 • La lettera è già stata scritta? Avrebbe dovuto essere stata spedita ieri.

USEFUL VOCABULARY
asta = *auction*
collezionista = *collector*
reparto vendite = *sales department*
riparare = *to repair*

8. LOST IN TRANSLATION? MIX IT UP!

Translate the following text into English using some of the words and expressions you have discovered in this story.

Avrebbe dovuto essere il lavoro perfetto, aveva perfino rifiutato un'offerta da Syntax, Inc. e deciso di non accettare altre due allettanti offerte di lavoro. Tuttavia, un recente imbarazzante incontro di feedback con la signora Miller, durante il quale era stata fermamente criticata, era stato la goccia che aveva fatto traboccare il vaso. Quando aveva iniziato questo lavoro, vi si era buttata a capofitto, cercando di dare un esempio alla sua nuova squadra, ma ora era pronta ad arrendersi, a buttare tutte le sue cose nel baule della sua macchina e andare a casa. Il tragitto verso casa non avrebbe portato via più di quaranta minuti, lì avrebbe potuto accendere il bollitore, afferrare un pacchetto di biscotti, infilarsi nel suo accappatoio e guardare i suoi film preferiti per tutta la notte prima di dormire troppo la mattina dopo... Ma poi il sogno finì, avrebbe dovuto partecipare a un'altra riunione tra dieci minuti, questa volta con Steve. Steve era snello e aveva un certo non so che, non voleva perderlo, forse questa volta sarebbe andata dritta al punto e lo avrebbe invitato fuori a cena... forse!

USEFUL VOCABULARY

allettante = *attractive*
criticare = *to criticise*
partecipare = *to attend*
perdere = *to miss*

Christmas

STORY 8

1 My name is Emma, I'm 41 years old. **It doesn't really matter** where I'm from, in reality I don't know anymore. The last twenty years of my life have been divided between two countries and two cultures, because I met, and later married, an Englishman. I met him twenty-one years ago, and since that day my world, and especially my habits, have changed very much. For example, I never used to drink tea, I only drank coffee, now I drink a minimum of three cups of tea a day: black with milk, no sugar. I also love fried eggs and baked beans for breakfast, it's my favourite!

2 Every single day of my life, even when I'm not in England, is a little bit English. What has changed more than anything else are my Christmas days. When I met my husband we started spending one Christmas at home (wherever home was, my husband's job has taken us all over the world) and one in England.
For my family the big day is Christmas **Eve**, when I was young we used to have a big party, with grandparents, aunts, uncles, cousins, great aunts, great uncles and second cousins, a total of twenty-four people. Things have changed over time and now we only spend Christmas with close family... eleven people! The only interesting part about Christmas with my family is when children open their presents. Otherwise nothing happens: we eat a lot and talk around the table for hours. It is pleasant, but sometimes it can be boring. In England it's a different story! The days are very **eventful**, let me tell you. One of the reasons is that my English family likes **to make fun of** each other. We all love each other deeply, but we joke a lot and sometimes English humour is a bit too much for me to understand! Last Christmas when we went to England, it was the most interesting holiday ever.
We've been travelling **back and forth** to England for about

eighteen years and Christmas journeys are always **particularly eventful**. In the past, there have been some occasions when we nearly didn't arrive in time for Christmas: once, years ago, it was simply the Christmas traffic. We're not talking about busy motorways, but for some reason the airports around Europe hadn't been able to keep up with the busy Christmas schedule. How is it possible that they weren't expecting thousands of people to travel over the Christmas period, it's not exactly a surprise, is it?

3 Last Christmas the problem was the snow. **A bit of** snow fell on London and everything stopped. I believe they use the word disruption in English to refer to these situations, and it really does give the idea. In my language, for example, they would use the equivalent of inconvenience: sitting in traffic for twelve hours at 4°C with no food or water (one of the common stories you hear in my country after a snowfall), is much more than an inconvenience, isn't it? Anyway, when we arrived at my husband's parents' house, there was no snow! **How disappointing!** Why does snow only fall on airports?

4 My husband's parents' house is big, there is space for everybody. There are three bedrooms, two are for guests and one is where my parents-in-law sleep. I have a problem with furniture and ornaments (which completely cover every available surface in the house): the house is full of them. They scare me, I must be careful every time I move and I am really worried about my children breaking something. The amount of cupboards, **chests of drawers** and **dressing tables** probably doesn't help, it's so easy to knock something over! I haven't told anybody, but a couple of times I've accidentally hit some pots, which then fell to the floor. I'm so, so happy my mother-in-law loves thick **carpets**: the pots bounced off without a single mark, scratch or **chip**... phew! I know I'm not the only one: once I saw my husband (who, **by the way**, is called Mark) dropping a vase that was hidden behind the bedroom curtain. He was also saved by the thick carpets. The children have been quite good too: they've used the ornaments for their cooking games, or for playing in the bath, but they haven't damaged anything... yet! The furniture is in strange places: in front of windows, across

corners... That's why in one of the bedrooms there isn't enough space for a bed. This means that Mark's mum and dad (Julie and Michael) sometimes let their guests use their room and sleep downstairs, on an **airbed**. That's what they did last Christmas, but there must have been a hole, because in the middle of the night they found themselves sleeping on the floor and finished their night on the **armchairs**. Their armchairs date back to the 1960s, and it's obvious... they might look nice, but you don't want to sit in them for longer than fifteen minutes, otherwise your **bottom** goes **numb**!

5 Before I start, I need to tell you something about our Christmas meals in general. Christmas dinner is normally at around 3.30 pm. It is early for a dinner, but you can't really call it lunch either, can you? The turkey normally spends all night cooking in the (gas) oven and the ham simmers all night long. I know what you are thinking. But don't worry, the turkey is fine in the oven on its own and the **simmering** water doesn't come out of the pot and turn off the gas... At least that's what they told me when they saw the terrified look on my face. Have you ever heard of an English house blowing up on a Christmas morning? No, exactly, so it must be OK... **fingers crossed**.

So, in the morning most of the meat is ready and cooked, only the lamb still needs to be prepared (so much meat!). There is also plenty of time to boil the vegetables and roast the potatoes. **Peeling** them is quick, even after a few drinks.

The gravy, the stuffing and the Christmas pudding (with double cream), only take a few minutes to warm up in the microwave. I love all the **shortcuts** we take when we cook our Christmas dinner in England. If my great aunt saw the instant gravy that we put on the turkey, she would scream in horror.

My parents-in-law have a different idea about stuffing to me. They prepare a pre-made bread mixture (from a packet), put it on the plate beside the meat, and call this stuffing. The word stuffing, which comes from to stuff, makes me think of filling something in, which means that the bread mixture should go inside the bird, not next to it! I was totally confused. Now I know: it is another shortcut! Take the mixture out of the packet, mix it with hot water, make it into a paste and **Bob's your uncle**! (Your uncle is not called Bob? Don't worry, we know. Check the idioms section.) What's the point in spending two days cooking, when you can make a decent meal in a morning and also have time to go to the pub? But I've never told my great aunt!

6 This year, on Christmas Eve, before going to bed, the children prepared a snack for Father Christmas and the reindeers. My husband told them "When I was a little boy I used to leave a glass of sherry, a small pie and a carrot for Rudolf". The children asked Mark what sherry was. "It's like wine..." Mark answered. They gave each other a **puzzled** look. Ok, how do you explain to them that Father Christmas isn't going to be completely drunk after he's visited all the children? My children know that drink driving is illegal "**Will Father Christmas get arrested if he drinks sherry and drives** his **sleigh**? Is that allowed?" At this point we decided to give him some milk instead. The tradition was broken, but we saved Father Christmas's life!

7 For children, Father Christmas is the best alarm clock in the world, and my children woke up at 6 am the following morning. Christmas day is the most important day of the year for them, how could we keep them in bed any longer? They ran downstairs to make sure Father Christmas had eaten his food and done his job. They were happy to see the presents, and were ready to open them immediately. However Mark's mum has a rule: we can open presents only when we are all together, but the grandparents were still in bed and we were also waiting for Mark's sister, Amy, and her family... it was only 6 am after all. It was very hard to keep them quiet: **Mark's dad's face**, when he came downstairs, told us he wanted to sleep longer, much longer. This was bad news, because he normally gets grumpy when he's tired. He decided to have a drink to feel better, a cup of tea of course, it was too early for a beer, even for him. The cousins arrived soon after (the Father Christmas alarm clock again) and they were allowed to open their presents.

8 After a light breakfast of sausage, bacon, egg, baked beans and fried mushrooms, we discussed whether to go to the pub for a

celebratory drink or to sit in the house... and drink. We all felt lazy and decided to stay at home, to cook (Mark and Michael), play (the children), watch television (Julie, Amy and her husband) or read (me).

At midday Mark and his dad were preparing vegetables and... drinking beer. Mark's dad started with potatoes, carrots, **turnips** and other vegetables that the children will never eat, Mark was **in charge** of peas, broccoli and brussels sprouts. It's going to be an enormous dinner, and as always, it was planned for 3.30 pm. The lamb was in the oven, how long had it been cooking for? It was an expensive piece of meat and Michael really wanted to cook it perfectly. I looked at the clock, I didn't realise it was so early. I had just finished thinking "We've got time for another drink. Time is passing very slowly, I know this book isn't very good, but it's not that bad," when...

Mark asked: "How long are you cooking that lamb for, Dad? It has been in the oven for more than three hours!"

Dad (Michael): "It's only one o'clock, there's still plenty of time."

Mark: "Are you sure? My watch says it's ten past two."

Dad: "Oh s**t! The clock has stopped."

Can you believe it? The clock chose Christmas day to stop working! The lamb came out of the oven immediately: dry, burnt, practically inedible. Not to mention the vegetables my father-in-law had prepared: the carrots were overcooked and the potatoes were burnt. He was destroyed, only another beer could make him feel better.

By half past two I had fallen asleep in front of the TV. I was woken up by screams from the kitchen and I immediately understood it was all about the broccoli. What happened? Mark walked out of the kitchen saying he didn't want **to have anything to do with** broccoli ever again. I followed him to understand more and try **to calm him down**. He hates overcooked vegetables, he believes that vegetables just need to look at boiling water and they are ready. When, one hour before dinner/lunch, Michael started cooking the broccoli, Mark decided that after the lamb, the carrots and the potatoes, he couldn't accept it, no more overcooked veggies were allowed. He asked his father what he was doing, and asked him if he realised that vegetables shouldn't be cooked like that. Obviously, a couple of beers earlier he would have been less direct, but it was too late. It was too much to take after his burnt lamb and Michael stormed off (a couple of beers earlier he would have been less **touchy**, but, again, it was too late). Mark followed him, trying to comfort him, but Michael didn't want to speak, he locked himself in the toilet, he was very angry. Julie and I tried to pacify the children... err, men... is there a difference? Luckily, by the time we sat down to eat, everything was ok, we all laughed and joked, popping our Christmas crackers... but there was no sign of any broccoli on the table. Was anybody going to say anything? They are the only vegetables my children eat, and I wanted them to eat some. At that point, Mark disappeared into the kitchen and came back with a pot full of broccoli, he put them on our children's plates, on his, and sat down to eat. Nobody moved, nobody said a word, they just kept their heads down and concentrated on their food: broccoli had become **unmentionable**. It was at that point that the children started screaming "Nice broccoli Daddy, really nice, can we have some more?" Everybody remained silent. To lift the tension, literally seconds after we had finished eating, Amy got up and started taking the plates away. "Does anybody want some Christmas pudding?" she asked, in an exaggeratedly happy and jolly voice. I was still chewing my last bits of lamb (it needed a lot of chewing), the children had broccoli on their plates. "Er, no thank you." Everybody declined the offer and, for the first time in years, we were saved from the super rich Christmas dessert. Nobody really likes Christmas pudding, do they?

9 I don't know how much television you can watch in one day, I surely didn't pass the BBC endurance test and soon went into the dining room with Amy for a chat and a drink. Our husbands joined us after a while and **we lost track of time**. We realised it was quite late when Mark's mum came in to tell us that our children were falling asleep on the sofa, but when she saw we didn't move (Christmas is for adults too, and it only comes once a year!) she stayed there with us, clearly ready to go to bed herself. Amy noticed it, and told her not to worry and to go to bed. At that point it was clear that the problem wasn't the children:

Julie asked us to leave the room so she could tidy up and close it before going to sleep. It didn't seem that untidy to me... Amy lost control "Do you think I'm not old enough to put four chairs under the table? You and your strange ideas, you are obsessed!" Please not again! Julie started to cry.
How much do you know about your mother-in-law? You probably only know what your partner told you, plus a few general things about their childhood. That's the closest you want to get to your mother-in-law, more than that can be dangerous. You enter the private zone, which, with mothers-in-law, must be avoided. Knowing something private about them could mean that they think you are becoming friends, they start giving personal opinions about your life and in the end you argue with them and destroy the relationship forever. That night Julie told all of us about herself, her feelings, her worries and fears. I know so much private information about her that if we ever argue we are never going to talk again! I'm my mother-in-law's friend!!!... How did I allow it to happen?!

10 The day was almost over, the children in bed, the grandparents in their old armchairs and the four of us still talking in the dining room. Were Julie and Michael really sleeping or were they pretending, making sure nothing was happening **behind their backs**? Mark whispered in my ear "How did it go, Emma?" Well, it went well. Definitely another unforgettable English Christmas, I really can't wait for the next one!

11 Emma sits down and gives the microphone to the man sitting on her right: now it's his turn to introduce himself to the new colleagues. What a strange thing to have to do during the first day of a new job. Talk about something personal, for 30 minutes, it was so difficult: she looks at the audience, at least they are still awake.

PRACTICE MAKES PERFECT

1. GOT IT? - Reading Comprehension

Answer the following questions.

1 • Why aren't Emma's origins important?

2 • What is the part about Christmas at home that Emma really likes?

3 • Why does Emma feel nervous in her husband's parents' house?

4 • Why isn't it possible for anyone to sleep in one of the bedrooms?

5 • What does Emma particularly like about how her parents-in-law prepare Christmas dinner?

6 • Why can't the children open their presents as soon as they wake up?

7 • Why did Michael burn the lamb and what did he do to reduce his disappointment?

8 • Why does Mark disagree with how his Dad cooks vegetables?

2. IN OTHER WORDS

Try to reword the following expressions, finding a synonym(s).

2 Christmas journeys are always particularly eventful =

3 A bit of snow fell on London =

6 They gave each other a puzzled look =

7 Mark was in charge of peas =

8 try to calm him down =

3. KEY WORDS - Vocabulary

Match the word with its definition.

2	eve	constantly moving or travelling between two places
2	eventful	a single, large, comfortable chair with supports for the arms
2	back and forth	a vehicle or platform pulled by animals
4	chest of drawers	a small piece broken from a hard material
4	dressing table	to boil gently
4	carpet	very sensitive and easily offended
4	chip	the day or period before an important event
4	airbed	cannot be spoken about
4	armchair	a shorter or quicker way of doing something
4	bottom	an item of furniture that consists of a table, mirror and drawers, normally used for getting dressed or applying make up
4	numb	an item of furniture that consists of a series of drawers
5	to simmer	the part of the body you sit on (buttocks)
5	to peel	a floor covering made of fabric
5	shortcut	a root vegetable, normally white and round
6	sleigh	full of interesting things or events
8	turnip	to remove the outer skin of a vegetable (e.g. a potato)
8	touchy	an inflatable mattress
8	unmentionable	without feeling

A BIT MORE...

IDIOMS/SLANG & MORE

The following idioms and expressions are used in the text, learn their meanings.

Where is it?	What is it?	What does it mean?
2	make fun of someone	*to ridicule someone and laugh at their expense* («prendere in giro qualcuno»)
4	by the way	*an expression to indicate that you are adding information* («a proposito»)
5	fingers crossed	*an expression that says you hope something happens or comes true* («incrociamo le dita»)
5	Bob's your uncle	*means "done!" or "everything is fine"* («fatto!, stai calmo, va tutto bene»)
8	to have something to do with something/ someone	*means to be associated with or connected to* («avere qualcosa a che fare con qualcosa/qualcuno»)
9	to lose track of time	*means to be unaware of what the time is or how much time has passed* («perdere la cognizione del tempo»)
10	behind someone's back	*without that person's knowledge* («alla spalle di qualcuno, dire o fare qualcosa senza che quella persona lo sappia»)

4. EXERCISE 1

Complete the following sentences using the idioms and expressions above.

1 • I hate it when someone talks about me .... back.

2 • You select tools, options, general settings then click "show profile pictures" and ...., your picture will appear the next time you log in.

3 • When Steve .... of people, he thinks he's being funny, but he's not, people find it irritating.

4 • Oh, ..., your husband called, he said it's nothing to worry about. He'll call back later.

5 • Damn, I ...., the meeting started 10 minutes ago and I'm supposed to be there.

6 • I'm having nothing .... this project, you just want everything done your way.

7 • The interview went quite well. They said that they'll call me by the end of the week to let me know, ...

EXTRA VOCAB – At the dinner table

When you go to dinner with your English speaking friends or perhaps your business colleagues, do you know what everything on the table is called? You probably know all the simple stuff, but look at the following image and learn some new vocabulary, this one has got a little Christmas twist...

1. Plate: *piatto*
2. Bowl: *scodella*
3. Cutlery: *posate*
4. Cup: *tazza*
5. Saucer: *piattino per la tazza*
6. Loaf of bread (on a cutting board): *pagnotta (su un tagliere)*
7. Christmas pudding: *dolce tipico di Natale, un tipo di torta a base di canditi, uvetta, spezie, mandorle e brandy*
8. Christmas crackers: *tipico di Natale, il Christmas cracker è un tubo di cartone avvolto da carta colorata, nella forma di una grande caramella. Tirandone le estremità, il cracker si apre emettendo un piccolo botto (da qui il nome cracker). Il tubo contiene una corona di carta, un biglietto con una battuta e un piccolo giocattolo.*
9. Gravy: *salsa, sughetto*
10. Serviette/napkin: *tovagliolo*
11. Wine glasses: *calice da vino, bicchiere vino*
12. Turkey: *tacchino*
13. Water jug: *brocca d'acqua*
14. Cheeseboard: *tagliere per i formaggi*
15. Vinegar: *aceto*
16. Toothpick: *stuzzicadenti*
17. Salt: *sale*
18. Pepper: *pepe*
19. Oven gloves: *guanti da forno*

Remember: in Inghilterra e in America non si mangiano il primo e il secondo. Spesso si consuma semplicemente un *single course* (piatto unico) che include tutto il pasto. A volte, specialmente al ristorante, il pasto è costituito da tre portate (a *three-course meal*) con uno *starter* (antipasto), un *main course* (piatto principale), e un *dessert* (dolce).

FOCUS ON...

IT DOESN'T REALLY MATTER (1)

It matters/it doesn't matter è un'espressione molto comune in inglese per dire se qualcosa sia importante o meno.

Esempi:
My son broke the kitchen tap, but it doesn't matter because we intended to buy a new one anyway. Mio figlio ha rotto il rubinetto della cucina, ma non fa niente perché avevamo intenzione di comprarne uno nuovo comunque.

"Come on, it doesn't matter, it's just a cheap ornament, nobody will care that it's broken." "Well, it matters to my Mum, she loves her ornaments!" «Dai, non importa, è solo un soprammobile scadente, a nessuno importerà che si è rotto.» «Beh, importa a mia mamma, lei ama i suoi soprammobili!»

FAMILY MATTERS (2)

Non preoccuparti! Non vogliamo annoiarti con una lista di parole riguardanti la famiglia che di certo conoscerai già, ma s'imparano sempre cose nuove e scommettiamo che ci sarà qualcosa di nuovo anche per te.
Vediamo un po'...

Great grandparents = i bisnonni! Si aggiunge semplicemente un *great* davanti al nome:
great grandfather (bisnonno), *great grandmother* (bisnonna), *great uncle* (prozio), *great aunt* (prozia), ecc.
Second cousins = cugini di secondo grado
Stepmother, stepfather = Quando i genitori si separano o uno dei due viene a mancare, ci si può sposare con un'altra persona. Se tuo padre sposa un'altra donna che non è tua madre allora questa donna diventa la tua *stepmother*. Se invece è tua madre a sposare un altro uomo, lui diventa il tuo *stepfather*.

Stepbrother, stepsister = Allo stesso modo se la tua *stepmother* o il tuo *stepfather* hanno un altro figlio nato da precedenti relazioni allora diventerà il tuo *stepbrother* se è un maschio o la tua *stepsister* se è una femmina.
Half-brother = Se poi dalla relazione tra tua mamma e il tuo *stepfather* (o viceversa) nasce un figlio allora lui sarà il tuo *half-brother* o, nel caso sia una lei, la tua *half-sister*.

HOW DISAPPOINTING! (3)

Questione di aggettivi: in -ING o -ED? Qual è la differenza?

Disappointing vs disappointed
Interesting vs interested
Boring vs bored

Questi sono solo alcuni esempi, che di certo conoscerai.
Ma sai davvero sempre scegliere tra un aggettivo in -ING e uno in -ED?
Forse queste semplici spiegazioni possono aiutarti:

-ING *describes a situation, person or thing*, descrive una situazione, persona o cosa; si tratta di aggettivi con funzione **attiva**, esprimono l'idea che qualcosa o qualcuno sia causa di un effetto;

-ED *describes how a person feels*, descrive come si sente una persona; si tratta di aggettivi **passivi**, esprimono l'idea che qualcosa o qualcuno faccia esperienza di un certo stato d'animo.

My exam results were very disappointing.
I risultati del mio esame sono stati molto deludenti.
Are you seriously interested in this film? I think it's boring.
Sei davvero interessato a questo film? Penso sia noioso.

GRAMMAR TOPIC: SAXON GENITIVE (POSSESSIVE S)

No, non ci siamo sbagliati! Abbiamo già parlato del genitivo sassone, ma questa volta aggiungiamo qualcosa in più...

7 *Mark's dad's face* = la faccia del papà di Mark

Due possessivi consecutivi, di seguito. È possibile? Certo: *George's dog's bone*. L'osso del cane di George.

Anche se non sono presenti nel testo, ci sono altri casi che fanno eccezione, ricordiamoli.
I sostantivi plurali irregolari, che quindi non finiscono per -S, seguono la regola di base: *the children's party* = la festa dei bambini.
Se due persone possiedono la stessa cosa, si aggiunge 'S all'ultimo nome: *Tony and Colette's car*. La macchina di Tony e Colette (la macchina è di tutti e due).

È anche possibile aggiungere 'S a un'intera espressione invece che a una singola parola:
The girl with the blonde hair's coat.
Il cappotto della ragazza con i capelli biondi.

GRAMMAR TOPIC: CONDITIONALS

6 *Will Father Christmas get arrested if he drinks sherry and drives his sleigh?*

È un esempio di classico **first conditional**. Per il bambino che ha posto questa domanda, il fatto che *Father Christmas* possa bere sherry e guidare la slitta è una possibilità futura e per eventi possibili nel futuro si usa il *first conditional*. Ricorda come si costruisce:

> *If clause* – *present simple*
> *Main clause* – *will* + forma base del verbo (o altri verbi modali al posto di *will*, es. *may*, *can*, *might*, *must*, *shall*, *should*)

If I make paella this weekend, I will invite Severine to join us for lunch.
Se faccio la paella questo fine settimana, invito Severine a unirsi a noi per pranzo.

If I go to London next week, I might visit my friend Mark.
Se vado a Londra la settimana prossima, potrei andare a trovare il mio amico Mark.

Il **second conditional** si usa per qualcosa che non è vero o per eventi futuri poco probabili.

If clause - past simple
Main clause - would + forma base del verbo (o altri verbi modali al posto di would, es. might, could)

If I were you, I wouldn't get involved in that project.
Se fossi in te, non mi farei coinvolgere in quel progetto.
If you won the lottery, you could buy me a villa in Spain with a swimming pool. Se tu vincessi la lotteria, potresti comprarmi una villa con piscina in Spagna.

Il **third conditional** è già stato menzionato in precedenza, ma questa sezione non sarebbe completa se non lo citassimo! Si usa per riferirsi a una situazione che è impossibile che avvenga perché già svolta nel passato.

If clause - past perfect
Main clause - would + have + participio passato (o altri verbi modali al posto di would, es. *might, could, can't, must + have* + participio passato)

If you had arrived earlier, you would have met my cousin Martin.
Se fossi arrivato prima, avresti incontrato mio cugino Martin.
If I had known you were coming, I could have organised a party.
Se avessi saputo che stavi arrivando, avrei potuto organizzare una festa.

Nota: non dimenticarti che esiste anche un altro tipo di condizionale, chiamato **zero conditional**, il più facile.

If clause - present simple
Main clause - present simple

Si usa per parlare di cose/fatti sempre veri a livello generale e universale oppure di situazioni sempre vere che si ripetono.

If I sleep too much I feel more tired than usual.
Se dormo troppo mi sento più stanco del solito.

Your eyes hurt if you look at the sun without sunglasses.
Ti fanno male gli occhi se guardi il sole senza occhiali da sole.

5. LOST IN TRANSLATION?

Use the above focus topics to translate the following sentences.

1 • Mia cugina di secondo grado è molto delusa della sua casa, pensa che la moglie di suo marito dovrebbe comprargliene una più grande.

2 • Se fosse andato a letto prima, probabilmente non si sarebbe svegliato così tardi. (*Clue*: prova a usare *might*)

3 • Sono così eccitato per la nostra vacanza, spero che la mia bisnonna non si annoi.

4 • I nostri pesci sono spaventati dal gatto della signora della porta accanto, ma quando gliene parlo lei dice che non importa.

5 • Il giardino della mia prozia è fantastico, trovo l'orto particolarmente interessante.

6 • «Jason, ti lascio, ho una relazione con il marito di tua sorella e siamo innamorati.» «Non mi importa, ora posso finalmente andare a vivere all'estero.»

7 • Il padre di Dennis gli hanno dato quel nome perché era il nome dell'amico del suo bisnonno.

8 • Il gol che hanno segnato ieri sera è stato sorprendente, ma sono stato più sorpreso dalle cheerleader!

9 • Se non smette di piovere, non possiamo andare in spiaggia.

10 • Se non lavorassimo per il Governo, avremmo più soldi.

USEFUL WORDS
Orto: *vegetable garden*
Relazione: *affair*
Segnare: *score*
All'estero: *abroad*

6. LOST IN TRANSLATION? MIX IT UP!

Translate the following text into English using some of the words and expressions you have discovered in this story.

La vigilia di Capodanno è sempre movimentata per mio padre, la mia matrigna e la mia sorellastra. Non ho più niente a che fare con le loro feste della vigilia di Capodanno, in passato sedevo semplicemente il mio sedere sulla poltrona e mi annoiavo. L'anno scorso hanno invitato l'intera famiglia, nonni, bisnonni, cugini, cugini di secondo grado, credo io sia stato l'unico che non era interessato a partecipare. Comunque, non mi piace parlare delle persone alle loro spalle, specialmente della mia propria famiglia, ma apparentemente hanno tutti perso la cognizione del tempo e hanno trascorso tutta la serata a bere. Avreste dovuto vedere la faccia della moglie di mio padre la mattina quando ha visto la confusione. C'erano persone che dormivano ovunque, su materassi gonfiabili, sul tappeto, una persona sulla toletta, c'era perfino qualcuno che dormiva sulla slitta in giardino. Quando lei vide che tutti i suoi soprammobili e piatti preziosi erano stati scheggiati rimase scioccata. Dopo aver trascorso trenta minuti correndo avanti e indietro cercando di pulire tutto, decise che non aveva senso essere delusa, «non importa» disse.

USEFUL WORDS
Intera: *whole*
Confusione: *mess*
Non avere senso: *to be pointless*

Saturday Night

STORY 9

1 I like Saturday nights. It's always the same routine, I know what is going to happen and I love that. At 7 pm I'm going to phone the taxi company and book a taxi for 8 pm, have a shower and put some nice clothes on, have something very small to eat and wait for the taxi to arrive. I'm going to arrive at the pub fifteen minutes later. Always the same pub, we've been going there for years, it's part of that chain which sells good **real ale** at sensible prices. I'm going to spend the next three hours there drinking beer with my friends and at about 11.30 pm I'm going to leave, go to the taxi office to book a taxi home and while I'm waiting for my taxi to arrive (that time of the night is **rush hour** for taxi drivers), I'm going to buy some dinner: pizza, kebab or some other **takeaway** from the shops in the area. At around midnight I'm back home, I have my dinner, watch some television and go to bed. A typical British Saturday night out.

2 I'm going to do the same this weekend: after today's match a friend from the football team asked me if I wanted to go out. My girlfriend is at her parents', so I really had no reason to say no. Appointment **set** for **around** 8 pm in the pub, as usual.
Tonight the pub is busy, there is nowhere to sit, so we decide to stand next to the bar. I don't feel like drinking beer, so **Miles and I** order a bottle of red wine to share between us. He's got a good reason to celebrate tonight, he's finally getting married! After all those years with Claire, they've finally decided **to tie the knot**! The wine is good, we hold our glasses and look at the empty bottle on the bar. Miles decides it's time to order another one: the night continues!

3 What is all this light in my eyes? My back is hurting. I open my eyes and look around. I'm on the sofa… I've slept on the sofa all night. Incredible! I always manage **to crawl** into bed, even when I've had too much to drink. The pizza box is still on the table, I could have a slice for breakfast with my tea… Yes, that's a good idea, if there is any left. I lift the lid and **I cannot believe my eyes**: the pizza is all there, completely untouched. I didn't eat it last night, not even a small bite. I'm shocked, it has never happened to me before, falling asleep on the sofa without touching my food! I can't even remember what happened. I'm definitely getting old.

I'm having breakfast, tea and cold pizza, lovely. My housemate, Justin, comes downstairs and sees me eating. **He was out with us last night, we have lived together for years**, but we never go or come back together. "Good morning mate, do you want a slice of pizza?" I ask him "I didn't eat it last night, can you believe it?" "Yeah, I know, you had quite a lot to drink last night, didn't you? I found you asleep on the sofa with the television on, I tried to wake you up but you didn't move, so I left you there."

I think about it for a few seconds "It's so strange, Miles and I only shared two bottles of wine, then I came home. I can normally drink much more than that." Justin looks at me "Really? What about what you drank in the nightclub? I didn't keep count, but I saw you with at least one huge cocktail in your hands." I'm not following now: nightclub, what nightclub? I only remember the pub and after that I came home in the taxi… didn't I? I actually don't remember that very clearly. I don't have any recollection whatsoever about anything after the pub. But I insist, "**You're pulling my leg!** I didn't go to the nightclub!" "Yes you did, there are many witnesses! All the boys saw you!"

Confronted with all this evidence, I decide **to give in** and accept his version of events. Justin explains everything I did the previous night, and I can't believe my ears. Apparently after the pub we decided to go to a local nightclub, there was a Latin American night. I took some dance lessons a few years ago, my ex-girlfriend was a ballet dancer and she couldn't stand being with someone who danced like a three-legged robot! I was pretty good, but we did jive dancing lessons, nothing to do with Latin

American. Apparently, I was the king of the dance floor, and apparently, I got involved in a dancing competition with a very talented Caribbean man. I'm glad he wasn't as competitive as me, because apparently I wouldn't accept that he was better than me. He was a big man apparently, but we settled the matter over a drink. I'm so disappointed that I can't remember, it sounds like it was **fun**. We spend the whole of Sunday laughing about my excessive **drunkenness** and my loss of memory and we wonder what else happened that we don't remember!

4 I don't like Monday mornings, you know, work and all that, but who does? I'm driving to work when my phone rings, **I pick it up**:
Miles: "Hello Daniel, it's Miles. How are you?"
Me: "Hi mate, I'm fine, you?" Miles's voice doesn't sound great.
Miles: "Yeah, not bad. Listen, I wondered if you could do me a favour..."
Me: "Yes, of course, no problem. What is it?" I ask him.
Miles: "You see, I had to go to hospital yesterday morning..."
Me: "Really? What happened?"
Miles: "I woke up on Sunday morning and my face was a mess: it was full of cuts and bruises. Something happened to me on my way home on Saturday night, but I was too drunk to remember when or where it happened!"
Me: "Oh yeah, we must have had quite a good drink on Saturday! I'm sorry to hear that." Miles carries on...
Miles: "Due to the seriousness of the injuries, the hospital automatically contacted the police and they are now investigating what happened. They are interviewing people who might know something about what happened that night and I gave them your name. Would it be possible for you to go and give a statement after work today, if you're not busy?"
Me: "Wow, that sounds **awful**, I hope you're OK. I'll go today, don't worry, I'll finish work early and go over there."
Miles: "Thanks a lot. As I said, I don't know what happened, but I suspect that someone beat me up, hopefully the police **will find out**."
We continue talking, he tells me that nobody took his money, his wallet or his phone, and he gives me more details about his

injuries. I hope he won't be left with any permanent **scars**. They wouldn't look very nice in the wedding pictures.

5 The police are waiting for me, an officer thanks me for coming, shows me to a separate office and asks me **to sit down**. He starts asking me questions about Saturday night, what I did, if I went past the station and so on and I tell him what I can remember, admitting that I had a bit too much to drink myself. I really start to feel under investigation myself, do they think it was me? Do they think that Miles and **I fell out** on the way home and had a **row**? Suddenly I realise that it could actually be true, perhaps I hit my friend hard and sent him to hospital and I can't remember. I start feeling **dizzy**. What happened on Saturday night? I need to find out.

6 **I'm lying down** on a doctor's bed. This is becoming a habit, for the second time in two days I **struggle** to remember where I am, but this time it **comes back** to me, this time I haven't forgotten. I **fainted** in the police station, after the questioning. "Don't worry Sir, it was nothing serious," the police nurse assures me, "To be sure we've taken a little blood sample to check your blood sugar level." I look at my finger tip and see a tiny red mark. "If you want, we can also perform more tests for further investigation." I know what happened, I started to think that a few drinks can transform me into a violent man and I collapsed, who wouldn't be shocked? I don't think I'll tell the police this. Anyway, I think why not, let's have these further tests.

7 I drive home, still unsure about what the police think of me, and what I think about myself. They said they are going to investigate and ask anyone who was near the station around the time we went home if they saw anything. **I dread to think** what they are going to find out. I get back and consider opening a bottle of wine, but **I put it back** in the rack: after the events of the last few days, I'm a bit **nervous** about what it can do to me.

8 At work today I'm very distracted, I can't focus. I'm sitting at my desk, I have a video conference call in about one hour but I can-

not face the thought of speaking to our Brazilian sister company's entire sales department. I make myself a cup of tea, the computer is already set to take the call, so I can sit at my desk and relax for a bit. **I sit back** and close my eyes, I must find a way to make myself feel better. Idea! Positive thinking! I'll start by singing one of my favourite songs, perfect! OK, I won't sing too loud, I don't want my colleagues to hear me... they would **take the mickey out of me** forever, I'm **such** a terrible singer. Holding my cup of tea, eyes closed, I try to relax while singing The Cure. Here I go, "I don't care if Monday is blue, Tuesday is grey and Wednesday too, Thursday I don't care about you, it's Friday I'm in love! Monday you can fall apart..." "Ahem!" I stop. Did I hear someone clearing their throat? I look around to make sure none of my colleagues heard me and I **turn pale** in horror. On my computer I can see the whole Brazilian sales department looking at me. What happened? Did I **inadvertently** start the call early? What are they doing there one hour early? I automatically check my watch... nooo, I forget I'm holding the cup and I spill hot tea all over myself. I jump up screaming in **pain**, it is at this point that I can hear the first **giggles**. Great, reputation destroyed! **I sort myself out** as quickly as I can and sit back at the computer, my shirt all **stained**, "Er, yeah, OK, I'm ready to start," I manage to say. "Last weekend we changed our clocks by one hour here in Brazil," the director explains, "I assumed you knew."

9 As soon as I leave work I switch my phone on: two missed calls. One is from Miles, the other from a private number.
"Hello Miles, it's Daniel," obviously I phone him straight away. "Hi, how are you? I got a call from the police," he tells me "they said the investigation has reached a conclusion." **My heart sinks**, "I'm going there now. Are you coming? Have they contacted you as well?" That must have been what the other phone call was. I confirm immediately "Of course, I'll see you there."
When I arrive at the Police Station I'm met by the same police officer from yesterday, he **escorts me into** an office, Miles is already there, he has just arrived. The police officer starts:
"Gentlemen, on Saturday night you were given sleeping tablets, they were probably put in your drink, everything else that hap-

pened is a consequence of this. You said you left your bottle on the bar: someone must have seen it and **spiked** it. We found high levels of a common sedative in your blood, some of its effects, when taken in high quantities, are loss of memory, heavy sedation, difficulties in walking, which you both experienced that night." He addressed Miles "We interviewed people who saw you outside the station but you were on your own, nobody **harmed** you. Your injuries occurred when you fell and crashed to the floor, without breaking your fall. The effects were probably worse for you because you are smaller than your friend."
The policeman is calling me fat! Anyway, I don't care. **I'm lost for words**, it's difficult to imagine something like this happening. I have a question now "Why would someone want to give us sleeping tablets?" "For some reason this is becoming a fashionable **prank**, it's a game young people are playing, there have been a lot of cases recently, they think it's **funny** but the consequences, as you have discovered, can be quite dangerous." Miles and I are **speechless**. It's shocking, how can people be like that! The policeman explains some more details, gives us some general suggestions for the future and we leave.

10 Before going home we exchange a few words in the car park "It's a bit **odd**, but at least we know that nothing serious happened." Miles says "Yes, I'm quite relieved, I was also quite worried about the effect that just a few drinks had on me, now I won't be afraid of that bottle of wine I've got at home, **fancy** sharing it with me?" We get back to my place and open the bottle of wine, "We should tell the boys about all this, and we should all go out again this coming Saturday night, to celebrate the happy ending." Good, we can **get back** to normality now. Boring, predictable, reliable Saturday nights, but now keeping our drinks **close by**.

PRACTICE MAKES PERFECT

1. GOT IT? - Reading Comprehension

Answer the following questions.

1 • Why was it impossible for Daniel to say no to going out?

2 • Why did the group drink standing up?

3 • What is Daniel's initial thought about why he slept on the sofa, left his pizza and can't remember anything?

4 • Why did Daniel's ex-girlfriend make him take dancing lessons?

5 • Why did the hospital phone the police?

6 • After his meeting with the police, why is Daniel so worried?

7 • How does Daniel realise that someone is watching him singing?

8 • Why are Daniel and Miles happy when they find out the truth about what happened?

2. IN OTHER WORDS

Try to reword the following expressions, finding a synonym(s).

2 appointment set for around 8 pm =

4 wow, that sounds awful =

7 I'm a bit nervous about what it can do =

9 he escorts me into an office =

10 but now keeping our drinks close by =

3. KEY WORDS - Vocabulary

Match the word with its definition.

1	real ale	to move using the hands and knees
1	rush hour	to suddenly and momentarily become unconscious
1	takeaway	a practical joke
3	to crawl	to have a mark on it or be discoloured
3	drunkenness	a little laugh
4	scar	to want something
5	row	traditional British beer, unpasteurized and unfiltered
5	dizzy	strange, unusual
6	to struggle	to be unable to say anything, normally through shock or surprise
6	to faint	argument
8	to turn pale	to add alcohol or a drug to someone's drink/food
8	inadvertently	the state of being drunk
8	giggle	to injure or hurt someone
8	stained	the period of the day when road traffic is at its heaviest
9	to spike	to have difficulty doing something
9	to harm	the mark left on the skin after a cut or injury has healed
9	prank	the sensation of spinning and feeling that you could fall
9	speechless	to lose colour in the face
10	odd	unintentionally
10	to fancy	a meal bought from a shop or restaurant and eaten elsewhere

4. FIND THEM OUT! - Phrasal Verbs Crossword

There are a number of phrasal verbs used in the text. They can be found in the paragraphs indicated below. Find the phrasal verb, match the context with the crossword clue, then add the phrasal verbs (infinitive form) to complete the crossword.

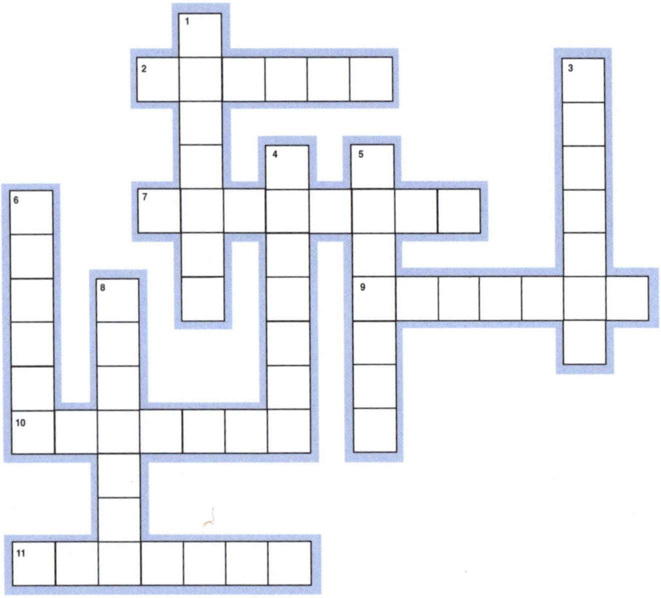

Across

2. To stop opposing and yield 3
7. To be remembered 6
9. To rest or be in a horizontal position 6
10. To return something to its original position 7
11. To lean against the back of the chair 8

Down

1. To discover 4
3. To sit on something 5
4. To return 10
5. To argue or disagree with someone 5
6. To answer the phone 4
8. To put yourself or something in order 8

A BIT MORE...

IDIOMS/SLANG & MORE

The following idioms and expressions are used in the text, learn their meanings and try the exercise that follows.

2 *tie the knot = to get married* («sposarsi»)

3 *I can't believe my eyes/ears = used when something is so surprising you can't believe what you are seeing or hearing* («non credo ai miei occhi/alle mie orecchie»)

3 *to pull someone's leg = to play a joke on someone by telling them something that isn't true* («prendere in giro qualcuno»)

7 *I dread to think = an expression that is used when you don't want to think about something because it is too worrying* («aver paura di pensare a qualcosa»)

8 *to take the mickey (out of someone) = to make fun of someone* («prendere in giro qualcuno») *in a lighthearted way* («in modo scherzoso, ironico, leggero»)

9 *someone's heart sinks = used when a person becomes very disappointed, discouraged or worried* («essere abbattuto, scoraggiato»)

9 *to be lost for words = to be so surprised or upset that you don't know what to say* («restare senza parole, non avere le parole perché si è troppo sorpresi o troppo delusi»)

5. EXERCISE

Complete the following sentences using the idioms and expressions above.

1 • My..............when the doctor told me I had diabetes.

2 • When the lottery company phoned to tell us we had won the lottery, I just couldn't........... .

3 • My girlfriend is always trying to convince me that we should......, but I'm happy with our relationship the way it is.

4 • I'm........, someone has scratched the side of our brand new car.

5 • "Please don't cut my hair Mum. If you do they'll take........ me at school."

6 • I .... what my dad will do to me when he finds out I've broken his fishing rod.

7 • I'm just........ your ...., I didn't really play professional football for Barcelona when I was young.

FOCUS ON...

MILES AND I... (2)

Questa è davvero una domanda supergettonata: si dice *Miles and I* oppure *Miles and me*? Chiariamo subito, è molto comune tra i madrelingua e nel linguaggio fluente parlato dire *Miles and me*, ma come puoi capire tu stesso *me* = pronome complemento e I = pronome soggetto. Quindi la forma corretta è *Miles and I*, anche se viene usata più spesso (ed erroneamente!) l'altra.

Esempio:
Mike and I are going to the pub to watch the rugby match, would you like to join us? Io e Mike stiamo andando al pub a vedere la partita di rugby, ti unisci a noi?

FUN vs FUNNY (3)

Due parole che mandano in confusione facilmente, ma è facile capire la differenza.
Fun è sostantivo e aggettivo (= divertimento, divertente, relativo al divertirsi, allo star bene).

Con funzione di sostantivo:
Come on, come to the beach with us, we'll have lots of fun.
Dai, vieni in spiaggia con noi, ci divertiremo un sacco.

Con funzione di aggettivo:
Thanks for inviting us for dinner last night, we had a really fun evening.
Grazie per averci invitato a cena ieri sera, abbiamo trascorso una serata davvero divertente.

Funny è aggettivo (= divertente, relativo al ridere o al far ridere).

Have you seen Dumb and Dumber? It's a really funny film. Hai visto Scemo & più Scemo? È un film davvero divertente (= che fa ridere).

SUCH (8)

Esempio: *I'm such a terrible singer.*
Such ha molti usi differenti in inglese; l'uso della frase presa dal testo è uno dei più comuni. In questo caso, infatti, serve per modificare e dare enfasi a un sostantivo graduabile, come se dicessi *I'm a really terrible singer.* Può essere usato sia con nomi *countable* che *uncountable.*

I've been such a fool, I should never have told her that I love her.
Sono stato talmente sciocco, non avrei mai dovuto dirle che l'amo.
I've never heard such lies! What is that politician talking about?
Non ho mai sentito simili bugie! Cosa sta dicendo quel politico?

PAIN (8)

In inglese ci sono molte parole per descrivere il male, il dolore (anche in italiano, in effetti!). Vediamone quattro in particolare.
Ache = un fastidio che continua per un certo periodo di tempo; non è di solito un dolore forte ed è spesso legato a una parte del corpo ben precisa: *earache, toothache, backache, headache* ecc.

This morning I woke up with a terrible headache.
Stamattina mi sono svegliato con un terribile mal di te sta.
Nota la pronuncia di *ache* = *eik.*

Sore = riferito spesso a qualcosa che fa male al tatto (non si tratta di solito di un dolore forte), oppure viene usato, per esempio, con espressioni come *a sore throat* (mal di gola), *a sore knee* (male al ginocchio) ecc.

Many people take antibiotics for a sore throat, but it's often a waste of time because most sore throats are caused by a virus not a bacterial infection. Molte persone prendono gli antibiotici per un mal di gola, ma è spesso una perdita di tempo perché la maggior parte dei mal di gola sono causati da un virus e non da un'infezione batterica.

Pain = un dolore, in generale. È certamente il termine più diffuso e di solito ha un'accezione più forte degli altri due. Può descrivere un dolore acuto o meno, di breve o lunga durata.

I keep getting a really sharp pain in my hip, I think I'll need to see a doctor. Continuo ad avere un dolore molto acuto all'anca, penso che avrò bisogno di vedere un dottore.

Hurt = fare male. A differenza degli altri termini visti sopra, è un verbo.

Does your neck hurt? I noticed you massaging it. Ti fa male il collo? Ho notato che lo massaggi.
You're hurting me, stop it! Basta, mi stai facendo male!

GRAMMAR TOPIC 1: STATE VERBS

3 *I'm having breakfast, tea and cold pizza...*
Sto facendo colazione, tè e pizza fredda...

Ci sono alcuni verbi che non ammettono la forma progressiva -ING, i cosiddetti verbi di stato. Sì, ma quali sono? C'è sempre molta confusione con questa -ING! Cerchiamo di far chiarezza.

La forma progressiva esprime sempre un processo in fase di svolgimento e può essere usata quindi solo con verbi che esprimono un'azione. Non a caso i verbi che contengono una -ING sono sempre detti *continuous*, continui. Sono dunque esclusi dalla lista i verbi di stato, appunto, quelli statici che di norma non esprimono nessuna azione.

• **Verbi di senso-percezione** = *see, hear, smell, taste* (di solito sono accompagnati dal modale *can*).

I can't smell anything, are you sure you burnt the cake?
Non sento (= odoro) niente, sei sicuro di aver bruciato la torta?

• **Verbi di opinione, pensiero** = *think, know, believe, understand* ecc.
I have known him for years. Lo conosco da anni.

• **Verbi di sentimento, volontà** = *love, like, hate, prefer, wish, want* ecc.
I want to call her right now, I need to ask her a very important question. Voglio chiamarla subito, ho bisogno di farle una domanda molto importante.

• **Verbi di possesso** = *have, possess, own* ecc.
I have a very bad headache, I think I'll go to bed to rest for a while. Ho un gran brutto mal di testa, penso che andrò a letto a riposarmi un po'.

• Altri verbi che non esprimono azione né movimento ma **stabilità e staticità**: *seem, be, mean, cost* ecc.
She means she doesn't want to come with you because she's too tired now. Lei vuol dire che non vuol venire con te perché è troppo stanca ora.

Ma (siamo ormai affezionati al "ma") è sempre vero? Questi verbi non ammettono mai la forma progressiva? Ebbene no, non è sempre vero. Alcuni verbi di stato, infatti, possono assumere un altro significato con il quale è ammessa la forma in -ING! Ecco alcune di queste eccezioni, le più comuni.

• **Have** = avere, possedere → **No** -ING, MA nelle frasi idiomatiche → **ok** -ING quando assume, cioè, significati diversi da «avere».

I have two brothers and five sisters, we're a really big family!
Ho due fratelli e cinque sorelle, siamo una famiglia molto grande!
Please don't bother me now, I'm having lunch.
Per favore non disturbarmi ora, sto pranzando.

• **See** = vedere → **No** -ING quando si riferisce al senso della vista → **ok** -ING se è usato nel senso di «incontrare, visitare».

Don't worry, I can see Peter playing with the other kids from the kitchen window, he's safe! Non preoccuparti, riesco a vedere Peter che gioca con gli altri bambini dalla finestra della cucina, è al sicuro!
They're seeing each other on Saturday so they can talk about the wedding. Si vedono (= incontrano) sabato così possono parlare del matrimonio.

• **Be** = essere → **No** -ING se ha il significato principale → **ok** -ING se usato nel senso di «comportarsi».

Betty is rude and I don't like the way she treats you.
Betty è maleducata e non mi piace il modo in cui ti tratta.

Betty is being rude, please tell her to stop and go home.
Betty si sta comportando da maleducata, per favore dille di finirla e andare a casa.

• **Think** = credere, ritenere, pensare → **No** -ING con questi significati → **ok** -ING se usato nel senso di «pensare, considerare, prendere in considerazione».

My father thinks my new boyfriend is a very polite person but a bit rough. Mio padre pensa che il mio nuovo ragazzo sia una persona molto educata ma un po' grezza.
I'm thinking about going abroad to study, it would be better for my future career. Sto pensando di andare all'estero a studiare, sarebbe meglio per la mia futura carriera.

Nota: potrà capitarti di sentire qualche verbo di stato usato nella forma progressiva, per esempio in canzoni, slogan, nel linguaggio parlato... sappi che è grammaticalmente scorretto!

GRAMMAR TOPIC 2: PRESENT PERFECT SIMPLE vs PAST SIMPLE

3 *He was out with us last night, we have lived together for years.*
Era fuori con noi ieri sera, viviamo insieme da anni.

Iniziamo con una definizione generale sull'uso di questi due tempi verbali.

Present Perfect Simple: azioni o situazioni connesse in qualche modo al presente.
Past Simple: azioni o situazioni avvenute in un certo tempo nel passato, compiute, concluse e finite, che non hanno alcuna connessione con il presente.

Prima di entrare un po' più nello specifico, nota che con l'espressione *in the last year* (= nell'ultimo anno, negli ultimi dodici mesi) si usa il *present perfect*, mentre con *last year* (= l'anno scorso) si usa il *past simple*.

PRESENT PERFECT SIMPLE	PAST SIMPLE
Azione avvenuta in un tempo indeterminato. È infatti sempre usato con avverbi o espressioni di tempo Indeterminati, non precisi: *just, already, yet, so far, never/ever, recently, it's the first* (second, third, ecc.) *time that* ecc. *I've worked too much recently.* Ho lavorato troppo recentemente *I've just met Mark at the supermarket.* Ho appena incontrato Mark al supermercato.	Azione avvenuta e finita in un tempo determinato. È infatti sempre usato in presenza di date precise (*in 1970* ecc.) oppure con avverbi o espressioni di tempo come *yesterday, last, ago.* Non è detto che il tempo sia sempre obbligatoriamente espresso nella frase, quando non è presente è sottinteso dal contesto. *I worked too much yesterday.* Ho lavorato troppo ieri. *I met Mark at the supermarket two days ago.* Ho incontrato Mark al supermercato due giorni fa.
Azione avvenuta in un passato recente che ha effetti nel presente. *She has broken her leg.* Si è rotta una gamba (la gamba è ancora rotta, non è ancora guarita).	Azione passata che non ha alcuna conseguenza nel presente. *She broke her leg.* Si è rotta una gamba (tempo fa, ma ora è guarita, non è più rotta).
Con espressioni come *today,* this *morning/month/year* ecc. quando il tempo non è concluso: *I've studied a lot this morning.* Ho studiato molto stamattina (è ancora mattina).	Con espressioni come *today, this morning/month/year* ecc. quando il tempo è concluso e finito. *I studied a lot this morning.* Ho studiato molto stamattina (adesso non è più mattina).

6. LOST IN TRANSLATION?

Use the above focus topics to translate the following sentences.

1 • L'Australia è un posto talmente bello, ci sono già stato quattro volte e ci tornerò l'anno prossimo.

2 • Ho mal di gola, mal di denti e male all'anca, oggi è un giorno così terribile.

3 • Quando passiamo la serata con Steve e Angela ci divertiamo sempre.

4 • Chris ha lavorato come commercialista nel 1999, ora vende tappeti.

5 • Hanno dei bambini talmente bravi, specialmente la più piccola.

6 • Ho questo mal di testa da più di una settimana, penso che sia ora di prendere un appuntamento per vedere un dottore.

7 • Sto pensando di andare in vacanza in Grecia, mio fratello c'è stato e ha detto che è bellissima.

8 • Ho talmente male a un polso, mi fa male ogni volta che provo a scrivere al PC.

USEFUL WORDS
anca: *hip*
mal di gola: *sore throat*
polso: *wrist*
scrivere al computer: *to type*

7. LOST IN TRANSLATION? MIX IT UP!

Translate the following text into English using some of the words and expressions you have discovered in this story.

Sono vicine di casa da quando erano bambine e durante quel periodo sono sempre state talmente buone amiche, ma è appena successo qualcosa. La situazione è in realtà piuttosto comica, tutto cominciò mentre Valentina era sdraiata a godersi una bibita quando improvvisamente iniziò a girarle la testa e sentì un forte rumore. Faticò ad alzarsi in piedi a causa del suo mal di schiena e del ginocchio dolorante, ma alla fine andò fuori carponi e vide che un grosso pezzo di plastica aveva colpito la sua macchina. "Strano", pensò, poi ebbe un tuffo al cuore. Guardò su e non riuscì a credere ai suoi occhi: un pezzo di plastica si era staccato da un armadio sul balcone della sua vicina, a quel punto la sua vicina uscì e cominciò la lite. Durante la lite Valentina impallidì di rabbia, finché alla fine la sua vicina si arrese, accettò che era colpa sua e promise di sistemare il danno all'auto. Poi si sedettero insieme e ridacchiarono della discussione che avevano appena avuto: «Quella era proprio una lite stupida, vuoi bere una bibita con me?» disse Valentina.

USEFUL WORDS
bibita: *drink*
forte: *loud*
alla fine: *eventually*
staccarsi: *to break away*
rabbia: *anger*
colpa: *fault*

Be
British English

The New Car

STORY 10

What happens if you talk to someone and you both don't realise there are communication issues? Do you think that English is only one language? See what happens when a Briton and an American try to strike a deal. Look at the following table, keep in mind these differences between British and American English and read the story!

British English	American English	Italian traslation	Note
pants	underpants	mutande	
trousers	pants	pantaloni	
momentarily	for a moment	momentaneamente, per un attimo	
soon	momentarily	presto, tra poco	
grey	gray	grigio	significato identico, spelling differente
pushchair	stroller	passeggino	
pram	baby carriage	carrozzina	in American English *pram* ha il significato poco comune di «piccola barca»
ground floor	first floor	piano terra	
first floor	second floor	primo piano	
petrol	gas	benzina	
gas	gas	gas	

British English	American English	Italian traslation	Note
handbrake	emergency/ parking brake	freno a mano	
driving licence	driver license	patente	da notare anche il diverso spelling nella parola *licenc/se*
cashier	teller	cassiere	un britannico probabilmente penserebbe che *teller* sia usato al posto di *fortune teller* («indovino»)
bonnet	hood	cofano	per un britannico *hood* significa «qualcosa che copre», per esempio un cappuccio
trunk	suitcase	valigia	
boot	trunk	portabagagli, baule	
football	soccer	calcio	
American football	football	football americano	
chemist's	drugstore	farmacia	
rubbish	garbage	pattumiera, spazzatura	

1 When I see it on line I know it's the one. It's only five months old, silver, beautiful. The car of my dreams at an unbelievable price. I've been checking this **second-hand** car website for weeks, it's always open in my browser, so I believe I'm the first one to see the **classified ad**. I reply without wasting a second.
"Hi BrownPants, is the car still available? I am interested in it. What condition is it in? Have you got any more photos? Thank you." Send.

2 Looking at the profile, BrownPants is a private seller, strange **nickname**, why does he need to tell people that he wears brown underwear? Why are his pants brown? No, I don't want to think

about it, disgusting! I just need to be sure that the car is in good condition, it doesn't matter what condition he's in. I know it's important to be careful when buying second-hand cars, especially from private sellers. I will make sure he's honest, that's what matters. I assume it's a man, with a name like BrownPants, surely if it were a woman the name would be BrownKnickers, wouldn't it?
I'm lost in my thoughts when the answer comes back. He's quick.
"Car available. Sorry, no photos."
He's a man of few words. The car hasn't been sold yet, perfect. According to the online map this person lives in Woking, only 30 minutes away. I'll go and see the car, I've decided.
"Thanks. Can I come and see it? When are you available?"
It's Saturday today, hopefully we can organize something for tomorrow... Oh, he has replied, already!
"Ok today at 1 pm? I'm moving away momentarily. Phone 07708 451094"
One o'clock is in one hour, this person doesn't waste any time. **Is he in a rush**? Why is it important that he's moving away? If it's only for a very short period of time, as he says, he will be back soon and we can meet another day. It doesn't matter, I'll phone him and clarify.
He answers immediately "Hello?". OK, he's a man. "Hello..." oh no, what do I call him now? "BrownPants?" "Speaking." "I'm contacting you about the car, I sent you a message earlier." I answer, he doesn't give me time to add anything else. "Yeah... meet ... Woking... one o'clock ... near football..."
I cannot hear him very well "Sorry, the line is breaking up, could you repeat please?"
"...no network ...low battery ...live near football pitch ...Woking. See you ...one o'clock. ...address is ...chester Road".
I listen and try to understand what he's saying. I'm taking notes, I've written down:
- Meeting at 1 pm
- Near a football pitch
- Address: ???
- His phone has no network and low battery

I didn't understand where he lives, I must ask or I won't find him: "Ok, see you at one. Can you send me your address please? I didn't quite **catch** that." "Ok... see you..." the line drops. That was

hard, I hope he has enough battery power to send me his address or my dream car will be gone forever.
He said something like ...chester, but what was the first part? My phone beeps, "my address: Leicester Road, Woking." I'm relieved, I can go and buy the car now! The address is not what I thought, it's Leicester, I must **have misheard** him.

3 OK, I check the map and get ready to go. He hasn't given me his house number, but with the road name and the other info I will find it: **there can't be many football pitches on this road**!
I drive my old green car and don't feel sad about the fact that I might be driving a new one soon. I will even have a **satnav**! I won't get lost anymore! **I don't get lost very often, but when I do I can deal with it on my own**. This is why I never ask for directions, it's just a matter of time before I find the right way. My ex-wife used to get very annoyed with me for this, she always wanted to ask for directions. Once we arrived late for a wedding, she was **livid**. It was her sister's wedding and she was the **bridesmaid**. I guess she had her reasons. Do satnavs save marriages? I wonder if we would still be together if we had a satnav back then.
Lost in my thoughts, I get to Woking **in no time**. This is the road, I've found it. Now I just need to find a football pitch. I **drive up and down** the road three times but I cannot see anywhere you can play football. The only place I could see that looked similar to a football pitch was a field behind a **fence**, with two tall white poles at each end, but from far away, it looked more like a rugby pitch. Er, I won't ask BrownPants, I'll go and have a look.
I cannot see any goals, this is definitely not somewhere where you play football, but there is nowhere else on this road. He must live here. Next to this "field" there are two buildings, they look exactly the same: which one is it? They have the same number, one is 197A and one is 197B, which one is it? I have no choice, I must phone BrownPants and ask.
Me: "Hello BrownPants, I'm in your road, what number do you live at?"
BrownPants: "Oh, hello. Good, it's 197, come in!"
Me: "OK, 197A or 197B?"
BrownPants: "I can't remember. The gray building."
Me: "Er, they are both grey..."

I have a look to spot any differences between them, but there aren't any. I notice something outside the front door of one of the buildings.
Me: "Is it the one with the pushchair outside the front door?" I ask.
BrownPants: "... pushing chair?" He's silent for a while "I don't think so, there aren't any disabled people living in the building."
He misunderstood me, I quickly change the wording.
Me: "No, no, I mean a pram!"
Silence again.
BrownPants: "I don't remember any boats."
This is not working.
Me: "OK, it doesn't matter, I'll come in and find you. Which floor do you live on?"
BrownPants: "First floor."
Me: "OK, I'm coming in."

4 I go into the building that is **slightly** closer to the field, hoping it's the right one. He said first floor, so I go up the stairs and look at the two doors. Which one is it? I have no option, I must knock on the doors. I knock on both doors at the same time. An old lady and a young girl open almost simultaneously, "Er... good afternoon" I say, "I'm looking for BrownPants". Oh no, what have I said?! The old lady **slams** the door in my face shouting "You **rude** man!" and the young girl looks at me "Have you ever looked at yours?" and closes the door behind her.
Clearly he doesn't live here, I'll try the first floor of the other building. I'm walking down the stairs when a door opens on the ground floor "Hi, are you here for the car?". "Yes, I am. Are you BrownPants?" I'm confused, I thought he said he lived on the first floor... "Yes, come in, the car's in the garage, I'll show you the documents first." I thank him, we go inside.

5 We start talking about the car.
Me: "Have you got the manual for the car?"
BrownPants: "Yeah!" I have a look.
Me: "**Does it consume a lot?**"
BrownPants: "No, it's not too bad for a gas car."
Me: "I didn't know it ran on gas, I thought it was a petrol car."
BrownPants: "Oh yeah, yes, petrol!"

What? Doesn't he know what his car uses? Strange.
BrownPants: "I'm not saying this because it's mine, but it's a very good car." He continues. "They say this model has a problem with the emergency brake, but I've never had any issues."
Emergency brake?! What kind of car is this? Has it got some sort of new safety device that I've never heard of?
Me: "Ah, ok" I say suspiciously, "so, how is this new emergency device installed in the car? How does it work?".
BrownPants: "What do you mean?" BrownPants is looking at me as if I come from another planet. "You got a driver license?"
Me: "Yes, of course I have got a driving licence!"
BrownPants: "So you should know what I'm talking about. You know, the brake you use when you park the car" he explains.
Me: "Ah! The handbrake!" I correct him. He's really strange, but I only need to understand if he's an honest person. I decide to change the subject to investigate this. "You said you are moving, can I ask why?"
BrownPants: "It's a love problem, I decided I can't stay here, I must go back home." He carries on "One day I spoke to a teller I know, and she said my girlfriend was going out with someone else".
A teller? Did he visit a fortune teller to find out what his girlfriend was doing? I'm curious.
Me: "How did she know?"
BrownPants: "She saw her, of course. She saw her with another man."
Did the teller see this in her **crystal ball**? Is he leaving the UK on the basis of that?
Me: "To be honest I've never spoken to a teller" I admit.
BrownPants: "What do you mean? You never spoke to a teller in your life?"
Me: "No. Never. Do you do it often?"
BrownPants: "Yeah, of course" he replies.
Me: "What do you talk about?"
BrownPants: "I don't know, it depends, we talk about stuff, I ask them questions, you know?" He seems surprised, it's his turn to ask questions now "How do you do that? I mean, not speaking to tellers?"
Me: "I don't know, I just do." I cut the conversation short. It's too **weird**, why can't we just have a normal conversation?

We go down into the garage to have a look at the car. **It's quite dark, I can't see much**.
"Do you want to open the hood?" BrownPants asks. The hood? Is it a **convertible**? Fantastic! **I've always wanted to own a convertible**, I'm so excited! He turns the light on and there she is: silver, gleeming, beautiful... but not convertible! Was he taking the mickey out of me? I look at him suspiciously while he lifts the bonnet and shows me a **brand new** engine.
This garage is large, there's a lot of stuff in it, big boxes, suitcases, and so on. He's ready to move, it looks like he's **packed** almost everything.
"Have a look inside the trunk, it's open." BrownPants tells me while I'm walking past a big case. I don't know why he wants me to have a look at his things, but I do as I'm told and open it: it is full of sports equipment, strange clothes, funny **helmets**...

6 Wait a minute, this man plays American football! Ahhh, now I'm starting to understand. Is that what that pitch was? I ask him and I understand that Matt (I finally find out his real name) came to England five months ago from the United States. He came here to play American football because his girlfriend was already living in the UK. They moved to Woking together, because this is where his team plays, but she started seeing another player from the same team. Matt found out one day while he was at the local chemist's (or drugstore, as he calls it), talking to a cashier who he knew because she was a big **fan** of his team. That's why he suddenly decided to abandon his - short - life in the UK, to sell the car he had bought soon after arriving and go back to the US **at once**.
I felt sorry for him. To lighten the situation, I try **to crack a joke**. "I hope your team mate is rubbish at American football, it would be really upsetting if he were good at that as well as getting women."
BrownPants: "Rubbish?"
Me: "Ah, sorry!"
I suppose if it's not possible to learn British English in five months, British humour is going to take a life time! And all the American films I've watched haven't taught me much either! Finally, I notice his brown leather trousers: a distinctive feature of a Texan, he tells me. We sit down with a beer and try to work out if we can actually understand each other while speaking the same language.

PRACTICE MAKES PERFECT

1. Ae vs Be

The following sentences are written in US English, change them into British English (some of the differences are not in the text, but they are commonly known so you may already know them – if not check out the table below).

1 • Let's go to the mall, put the shopping bags in the trunk of the car.

2 • The train will arrive momentarily, our vacation is about to start.

3 • When you stop the car in the gas station you should always put the emergency brake on.

4 • I told the teller in the store that I didn't want to buy the packet of cookies.

5 • It's normally a good idea to put your underwear on before you put your pants on, if you do it the other way round people might laugh at you.

6 • I drove on the freeway in a gray car that didn't have a hood, when the police stopped me they asked me for my driver license.

7 • When you get to the parking lot, can you put the garbage in the trash can please?

8 • I've been playing soccer ever since I got out of the stroller.

EXTRA WORDS

British English	American English
shopping centre	mall
holiday	vacation
shop	store
biscuit	cookie
motorway	freeway
car park	parking lot
rubbish bin	trash can

2. KEY WORDS - Vocabulary

Match the word with its definition.

1	second-hand	a familiar name that substitutes a person's real name
1	classified ad	to shut something (e.g. a door) very firmly
2	nickname	a glass ball used by fortune teller to see into the future
2	to mishear	a structure (made of wood, for example) that encloses an area (e.g. garden)
3	livid	protective equipment for the head
3	bridesmaid	a small and short advertisement in a magazine or newspaper
3	fence	a person who follows and supports a person (e.g. pop star) or team (e.g. sports team)
4	slightly	strange
4	to slam	to put some things in a bag, suitcase or other type of container
4	rude	a person (female) who assists and accompanies a bride at their wedding
5	crystal ball	not new, has had a previous owner
5	weird	to a small degree
5	convertible	to fail to hear something correctly
5	to pack	impolite or insulting
5	helmet	a car that can be converted by removing the roof
6	fan	very angry

A BIT MORE...

IDIOMS/SLANG & MORE

The following idioms and expressions are used in the text, learn their meanings try the exercise that follows.

Where is it?	What is it?	What does it mean?
2	to be in a rush	*when you don't have much time and so you must do things quickly* («aver fretta, andare di corsa»)
2	to catch	*the common meaning of this word is to get and hold something in the hand (something thrown or dropped, e.g. a ball), but here it has a different meaning, it simply means to hear* (di solito significa «prendere, afferrare», ma in alcuni casi, come nel testo, vuol dire «capire, afferrare le parole»)
3	satnav	*short for "satellite navigation system" and is now the common name used for the GPS route devices used in cars* («navigatore satellitare»)
3	in no time	*very quickly* («in men che non si dica, velocemente»)
5	brand new	*a term that underlines the fact that something is completely new* («nuovo di zecca»)
6	at once	*immediately* («subito, immediatamente»)
6	to feel sorry (for someone)	*to feel sympathy for someone because they are in a difficult or sad situation* («essere dispiaciuto, per qualcuno». Ricorda che *sympathy* è un *false friend* e significa «affetto, empatia, compassione»)
6	to crack a joke	*another way of saying "to tell a joke"* (un modo un po' più informale per dire «fare una battuta» o «raccontare una barzelletta»)

3. EXERCISE

Complete the following sentences using the idioms and expressions above.

1 • Don't................ or me, it's my fault that I lost my job.

2 • I'm always the one .... at dinner parties, but some people don't find me funny.

3 • I can't talk right now, I'm...................., can I call you back tomorrow?

4 • I've just bought a....................... car and I've scratched it already, I should have followed my son-in-law's advice and bought a second-hand one.

5 • Get out of my office........................, if you are still here when I count to ten, I'll sack you.

6 • Once the book was published it sold 10,000 copies................. at all.

7 • It was a bad line so I didn't........................ what he said about next week's meeting.

8 • If you had remembered to bring the........................, we would have arrived on time.

FOCUS ON...

DRIVE UP AND DOWN... (3)

È abbastanza comune usare *up* e *down* con verbi quali *drive*, *walk*, *run* ecc. che descrivono l'azione di muoversi lungo una superficie piana.
If you drive up the street and turn right at the end, you'll see the cinema in front of you. Se prosegui (in auto) lungo la strada e giri a destra alla fine, vedrai il cinema di fronte a te.

Dato il significato proprio delle parole in questione, ci si può confondere facilmente e pensare che chi usa *up* e *down* stia parlando di una collina o di una discesa, ma non è necessariamente così.

OWN (3)

Stessa parola ma due significati completamente diversi.

3 *I don't get lost very often, but when I do I can deal with it on my own.*

On my own (or on one's own) = per conto proprio, stare da soli oppure fare qualcosa senza l'aiuto di nessuno.

Nobody can believe that I built this house on my own, but it's true, I did everything myself. Nessuno riesce a credere che ho costruito questa casa da solo, ma è vero, ho fatto tutto da me.

My wife and daughter left to go and live in Australia, and I've been on my own ever since. Mia moglie e mia figlia sono partite per andare a vivere in Australia e sono rimasto da solo da allora

5 *I've always wanted to own a convertible.*

In questo caso to own = possedere, avere.

I have never owned my own house.
Non ho mai avuto/posseduto una casa mia (di mia proprietà)

Oops, guarda un po', c'è anche un terzo significato! In questo caso own è usato con un pronome possessivo per enfatizzare il fatto che qualcosa appartiene a qualcuno.

The German Shepherd is their own dog, but they are also looking after their neighbour's two dogs, that's why they've got three. Il pastore tedesco è proprio il loro cane (= appartiene a loro), ma stanno badando anche ai due cani del loro vicino, ecco perché ne hanno tre.

GRAMMAR TOPIC 1: MANY/MUCH vs A LOT OF

3 There can't be many football pitches on this road.

5 Does it consume a lot?

5 It's quite dark, I can't see much.

Te li presentiamo: i **quantifiers**!
Nice to meet them? Vediamo come si usano prima di dirlo...
Innanzitutto chiariamo la questione *uncountable/countable*:
Many si usa con nomi *countable*
Much si usa con nomi *uncountable*
A lot/lots of si usa con nomi sia *countable* sia *uncountable*.

OK. Ora per renderla più semplice cerca di ricordare una cosa importante:

MUCH e MANY sono generalmente usati solo nelle frasi negative e interrogative.

Detto ciò, tutto il resto va bene!

Gli esempi presi dal testo si sarebbero potuti scrivere in modo leggermente diverso ma sarebbero stati ugualmente corretti:

There can't be many football pitches on this road.
There can't be a lot of football pitches on this road.

Does it consume a lot?
Does it consume much?

It's quite dark, I can't see much.
It's quite dark, I can't see a lot.

Nota: nel secondo e nel terzo esempio non viene usato nessun sostantivo e quindi *of* si deve omettere. Quando invece è presente il sostantivo, si usa *a lot of* (non solo *a lot*).

Per esempio: *We've got a lot of butter in the fridge.*

E se consideriamo la regola detta precedentemente, allora la seguente frase non può essere cambiata:

I've got a lot of money.
~~*I've got much money.*~~

GRAMMAR TOPIC 2: THE PRESENT PERFECT SIMPLE IN US ENGLISH

Notate qualcosa di strano nelle frasi seguenti?

Me: "To be honest I've never spoken to a teller" I admit.
BrownPants: "What do you mean? You never spoke to a teller in your life?"

Abbiamo parlato tanto delle differenze **Ae vs Be** nei vocaboli, nello spelling, nella pronuncia, ma le diversità ci sono anche nella grammatica!
Nel linguaggio colloquiale comune, infatti, molti americani non si attengono alle regole rigide del **Present Perfect** e usano molto spesso il **Simple Past** anche dove, secondo l'inglese standard, non si dovrebbe!
È sempre utile saperlo, no? Così non penserai di essere impazzito, ma saprai da dove ha origine la confusione.
Vediamo qualche esempio...

UK – I don't feel well, I think I've eaten too much.
US - I don't feel well, I think I ate too much.

UK – I'm not going to the cinema tonight, I've already seen that film.
US - I'm not going to the cinema tonight, I already saw that film.

UK – Have they decided who's going shopping yet?
US – Did they decide who's going shopping yet?

4. LOST IN TRANSLATION?

Translate the following sentences using the "Focus on" and "Grammar" topics.

1 • Abbiamo molte uova in frigo.

2 • Ho sempre voluto dirigere una mia propria azienda, ma hai bisogno di molti soldi per l'investimento iniziale e non ne ho molti.

3 • Ho passato anni a guidare la macchina di mio padre, quando ho comprato la mia (= propria) ero così fiero che l'ho guidata su e giù per la strada per giorni.

4 • Parlante britannico: «Wow! Hai il nuovo DVD di Tarantino. Posso prenderlo in prestito, per favore?» Parlante americano: «No, non l'ho ancora visto.»

5 • Edward ha fatto questa torta da solo, ha solo nove anni, molti bimbi della sua stessa età non lo saprebbero fare.

6 • «Quanta acqua dovresti bere ogni giorno?»
«Non sono sicuro, ma è molta.»

7 • Se vai lungo il sentiero, attraverso il cancello, giri a sinistra e poi cammini su per la strada, troverai il supermercato dopo circa 300 metri.

8 • «Da quanto tempo hai (=possiedi) uno yacht?» «In realtà non ho un mio proprio yacht, ho solo un'agenzia che li vende.»

USEFUL WORDS
Dirigere: *to run*
Fiero: *proud*
Prendere in prestito: *borrow*
Cancello: *gate*

5. LOST IN TRANSLATION? MIX IT UP!

Translate the following text into English using some of the words and expressions you have discovered in this story (doesn't include differences between US and UK English).

Non ha mai avuto (=posseduto) il suo proprio violino perché non aveva molti soldi e non potrebbe permettersene uno nuovo di zecca. Un giorno, mentre stava camminando lungo la strada, vide un violino di seconda mano in una vetrina, se ne innamorò subito e, nonostante costasse molti soldi, sapeva che doveva averlo. Era di corsa visto che stava andando in vacanza e non aveva ancora fatto le valigie. Corse giù per la strada, saltò sopra una cancellata e spinse un po' di persone che facevano shopping, sapeva che era da maleducati ma non ne era dispiaciuta, tutto ciò che le importava era il violino. Saltò sulla sua macchina decappottabile, sbatté la porta, mise su il suo casco (faceva molta attenzione alla sicurezza) e guidò lungo la strada, doveva arrivare a casa per prendere i soldi per il violino. Accese il navigatore e arrivò a casa in men che non si dica, ma quando entrò in casa non poteva credere ai suoi occhi, la sua casa era stata svaligiata. I suoi soldi, il suo passaporto, la sua borsetta, tutto andato. Voleva fare una battuta per sentirsi meglio, ma sapeva che sarebbe stato strano, così restò lì seduta, a dispiacersi per se stessa e pianse... niente battute, niente vacanza, niente violino.

USEFUL WORDS
Persone che fanno shopping: *shoppers*
Svaligiare: *to burgle*
Permettersi (economicamente): *to afford*
Borsetta: *purse*

Solutions

1. THE AMERICAN DREAM

1. GOT IT?

1 • The word Mary could not understand was "though".
2 • They lit a fire and had marshmallows with chocolate.
3 • Chocolate and peanut butter.
4 • She took Latin at school.
5 • She really liked it, her Latin teacher was very funny and nice.
6 • She won a box of peanut butter cups.
7 • She felt sick because she got chicken pox.
8 • Her American uncle helped her when she was sick because he was a doctor.
9 • He asked what her full name was and she thought he asked for her phone number!
10 • He played the guitar and sang a song for her.

2. IN OTHER WORDS

I'm now 40 years old.
a lot of times.
Can you imagine me there?
we all became friends, we all had a nice relationship
The important thing was the fact we were there

3. KEY WORDS

aware = conscious of; lazy = the opposite of a lively and active person; dumb = stupid; to figure out = think, realize; adjust = adapt; laundry = clothes to be washed; fun fair = amusement park; junk food = unhealthy food; pimple = a small spot on the skin; chicken pox = a disease with marks on the skin; to pretend = to deceive, make believe; stuffed = filled with something; deaf = unable to hear; to whisper = to speak with a soft low voice; daydreaming = fantasize, dream with open eyes; staring = looking at deeply, having a fixed look at something or someone

4. FIND THEM OUT!

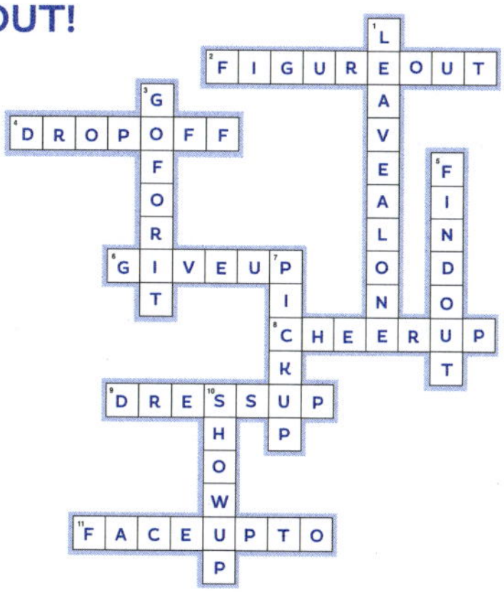

5. LOST IN TRANSLATION?

1 • My flight was delayed because the plane was damaged, thank goodness I was not alone and I arrived home safe and sound!
2 • Ugo is not good at English, but it doesn't matter, he can cook very well!
3 • I couldn't stand him in the beginning then I had a crush on him and we're getting married next year.
4 • Come on, it's not a big deal! You have been fired but another company has called you already. See? You are lucky! Always look on the bright side.
5 • We have done a great job so far, they are all satisfied with the results that have been achieved.

6. LOST IN TRANSLATION?

1 • Kris is the most beautiful girl in this office, but she's not the nicest.
2 • The best thing you can do is to call everybody but him, then he'll understand you're angry.
3 • Even though this exam was easier than the last one, Tom still did it all wrong.
4 • My new kitchen is as big as hers, but she still thinks hers is better.
5 • He's the most polite/politest man I've ever met, I want to marry him!

7. LOST IN TRANSLATION? MIX IT UP!

I've just turned fifty, I'm getting older and older... and also a bit deaf! People always seem to whisper words and I don't understand them. But I don't give up and I pretend to smile. My cousin was good at inventing new mottos, my favorite one was: "Dress up and cheer up!". I would also like to add "eat some junk food", it doesn't matter if it's not healthy, sometimes it's good for your mood! See? I can give up everything but my irony! Fifty years old and so far so good, I got here safe and sound.

2. WHAT A HOLIDAY!

1. GOT IT?

1 • Frank and Nick had just finished their first year of University.
2 • Frank fell in love with the French teacher.
3 • They chose to go to Barcelona because Frank had some relatives there so it would have been cheaper than other places.
4 • The air conditioning didn't work.
5 • They argued about money.
6 • He had the soy soup because Nick forced him to order it, making fun of him with the barman.
7 • Because he heard the phone ringing but they didn't have a phone!
8 • It was a street light.
9 • They were asked to pay 20 euros each but then they negotiated and paid 30 for both.
10 • They couldn't rest, Frank's cousin insisted on going to the seaside.

2. KEY WORDS

to lend = to give something to someone on condition that it will be returned; to drag = to pull something/someone slowly and with difficulty; boardies = bathing suit; fan = an object you can wave with your hands to move the air around you when it's too hot; flip flop = a flat sandal, usually used in the summer; scatterbrain = a foolish person, someone who forgets things; relieved = feeling glad, no more anxiety, no worries; veggie = someone who doesn't eat meat; still (adj.) = stationary, not moving; weird = strange; to deserve = to be worthy of, to merit; naïve = innocent; flashing light = something bright that keeps going on and off; penny-pincher = someone who cares about money too much; hood = the part at the front of a car, covering the engine; to dump = to leave, break up, let fall; change (n.) = the money you give in return when someone paid you more than needed; disappointing = when something or someone has not met your expectations; dinghy = a small inflatable boat;

3. GUESS

to fall in love with someone = to be in love with someone; to invite someone over = to invite a person/people to your house; to mess it up = to make untidy, confuse, to disorder; to sort things out = to solve, find a solution to; to break up with someone = to separate, to put an end to a relationship

4. LOST IN TRANSLATION?

1 • Guess what? If you break up with me I'll be happy because you've always been a penny-pincher! How did I manage to fall in love with you?
2 • I've invited them over so they can bring Steve who is a hunk of a man and I can introduce him to my cousin.
3 • If I could I would wear flip-flops all day, even at work, I can only take a fan instead.
4 • I don't know what happened, but I lost my mind and I messed it up. I've just had a steak but I'm a veggie!
5 • I feel relieved, my six children are recovering from the flu.
6 • My brother is so naïve that he never argues with anyone about anything.

5. LOST IN TRANSLATION?

1 • Tomorrow's meeting is at 7.00 in the morning. You'll pick me up, won't you?
2 • My uncle always wins when we play cards but we're finally even now.
3 • My father's cousin's son lives in Madrid.
4 • "What time are you coming back tomorrow?" "Well, actually... I'm not leaving anymore!"
5 • She does wear glasses! I'm sure of it, they're yellow!
6 • Milan's cathedral is wonderful, but I prefer the Sagrada Familia in Barcelona.
7 • I can't remember the name of the street that Mike's house is on, can you?

6. PRONUNCIATION EXERCISE

Finished - t; Decided - id; Started - id; Organized - d; Invited - id; Used - d; Deserved - d; Agreed - d; Packed - t; Planned - d; Tried - d; Shouted - id; Called - d; Added - id; Stopped - t; Looked - t; Dragged - d; Interrupted - id; Remained - d; Wished - t;

3. A SLEEPLESS NIGHT

1. GOT IT?

1 • They are usually richer, healthier and funnier than skinny ones.
2 • He comes from France.
3 • They all call him uncle Tony, after the name of their favorite Italian restaurant.
4 • He thought she said "prosecco", the Italian wine, but she said "Prozac", the antidepressant pill.
5 • Because he had too much lasagna for dinner.
6 • He starts writing a letter to the love of his life.
7 • He has to bring some food to entertain the clients and give Mike more time to find his presentation.
8 • He usually starts them with a funny story to catch the audience's attention.
9 • He decides to quit his job.
10 • Five years.
11 • He passed out because Maggie confessed she's engaged to Rob, Mike's best friend at work.

2. KEY WORDS

very thin = skinny; happy = cheerful; to test the flavor of something by eating or drinking = to taste; crazy = nuts; filled with something = stuffed; free from hair, not rough = smooth; nude, with no clothes = naked; to hurry = to rush; confused = puzzled; the people present at a meeting/conference = attendees; to please someone by compliments or attention = to flatter; to quit/give up your job = to resign; man's formal dress = tuxedo; to annoy, to cause someone trouble = to bother; cold = chilly; not soft, strong, hard, difficult = tough; a person that often changes his/her feelings (happy, sad, etc.) = moody; to plan to get married = to be engaged; more than just a boyfriend/girlfriend, someone who is due to get married = fiancé; to slide = to slip; to close and open one eye quickly, it is often done as a signal = to wink.

3. FIND THEM OUT!

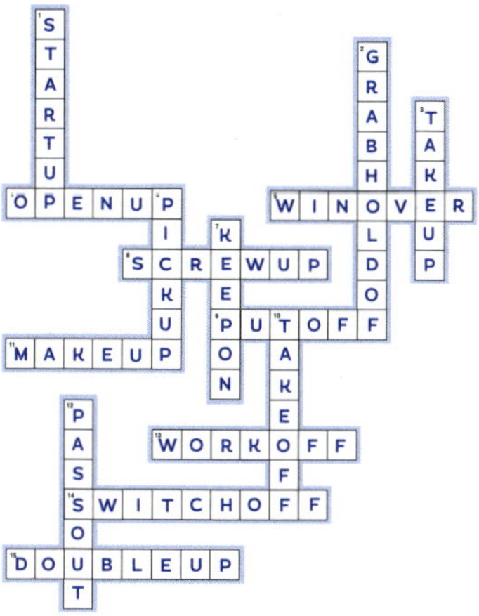

4. LOST IN TRANSLATION?

1 • Jack fell head over heels with me, I'm flattered but it wasn't love at first sight for me. I think I'll make up an excuse to break up with him.
2 • Lisa is really beautiful, she winked and she won me over! We're engaged now and we're getting married in June, 2030.
3 • "I've just taken up golf, I like it very much." "Didn't you want to take up tennis?" "Yes, but the teacher was too moody so I gave up."
4 • "I have to work off my anger, I decided to resign, wish me luck." "Please don't pass out in front of your boss as you always do! Couldn't you just take some days off as everybody does?"
5 • There were a lot of attendees at the conference, I had prepared a very important speech, but I screwed up everything! I felt too much anxiety and I started to stutter." "Buddy, come on, don't sweat the small stuff, I'm sure they didn't think you're nuts, but just very shy."
6 • "I'm sorry to bother you, but my husband would like to taste your famous chocolate cake. Can you please give me the recipe?" "Sure, no problem! I didn't know he liked sweet food, he's so skinny!" "You're right, who knows how he doesn't put any weight on!"

5. LOST IN TRANSLATION?

1 • Everywhere I go, I always get lost and I have to stop and ask for directions because I don't have a GPS in my old car.
2 • If I were him I would get very angry, they are supposed to get married in two days and she has just broken up with him!
3 • It's raining, you'd better not get wet or you'll get the flu again!
4 • I'd rather not go out tonight, I have to get up very early tomorrow morning, I have an important meeting at work.

5. She'd better go to Patty's party, even if she'd rather have dinner with us because I made her favorite dish.

LOST IN TRANSLATION? MIX IT UP!

My brother and I started up a new business, we sell sportswear online. We created a fantastic new website and we are doing a roaring trade! Who knows if it will always be so successful, let's hope so. We meet a lot of people for work because we need to buy the products and discuss costs. I met this beautiful smart girl the other day, she's driving me crazy, I always think of her. Thanks to her I never get bored at work and I always find an excuse to call her. My brother says she's a psycho, just because her mood often changes but I think this is just the way all girls are. I could have any girl I want but I only want her. If I were braver I would write a love letter to her, even if it's old fashioned. "You'd better stick to work and forget about that girl", this is what my brother keeps telling me. He doesn't like her, he thinks she's skinny, but I don't care, we have different tastes. The phone rings: "Am I bothering you?" I hear her voice speaking, what a nice voice... "Of course not! You never bother me." "I just wanted to tell you that I've decided to resign, I've found a better job. It's been nice working with you and I wish you all the best." "Hem, ok, but you'd better come and see me before you quit." So this is the end, I thought, I'd rather spend the rest of my life in prison than never see her again! I'm going crazy, I absolutely have to see her. And here we are, two years later, happily married.

4. A DOG'S LIFE

1. GOT IT?

1 • His sister Linda calls him, because she lost Arthur, her dog.
2 • Because he says that it is only a dog after all, but it's like a son to her.
3 • No, he thinks Andy makes fun of people and lies to them just to get what he wants.
4 • She works in a bank, but she wanted to be a writer or an artist.
5 • They're from Mexico.
6 • He talks to the old Mexican lady, but he doesn't get much out of her, only a statement that sounds like a prophecy.
7 • He calls his Egyptian baker, Philip, to help him with burritos, because he promised them to Linda's neighbor when he was trying to convince the old lady to speak to him.
8 • He finds Arthur's leash.
9 • She says Bob needs a fireplace, because her Indian friend Albert buys and sells fireplaces.
10 • Bob finds Arthur in Albert's basement, Albert's daughter was bathing the dog, cuddling him.

2. KEY WORDS

stubborn = someone who never wants to change opinions, obstinate; frantic = desperate, agitated; whining = complaining, making a long and sad sound; regretted = felt sorrow and unhappy with something done; (to) report = to tell the police; to downplay = to minimize, not to give much importance to something; (to) blame = to say that someone is responsible for something; crowded = full of people; avoided = stayed away from something; paranoid = it describes a person suffering from paranoia; envious = when you desire someone else's life/things; mangy = dirty, unclean; chubby = quite fat, round and plump; wrinkles = lines or creases on your skin, they usually appear when you get old; a stern gaze = a strict/severe look; bewhiskered = having hairs around the mouth; leash = something you use to control and lead a dog or another animal; fence = something used to mark borders, a barrier; walk-in-closet = a place you keep your clothes that is big enough you can walk in it; neat = clean, tidy; purebred = an animal of pedigree; a studio apartment = a one-room apartment; chatty = someone who talks a lot, talkative; (to) pop = to come or go quickly; chicken (adj.) = scared, not brave, not courageous; clear-headed = free from other worries or thoughts, calm; marital breakdown = a period of crisis for a married couple; lovebirds = a pair of lovers; basement = the part of a house that is underground; kidnapping = stealing someone, usually as a hostage, to get money; cuddling = hugging, embracing;

3. FIND THEM OUT!

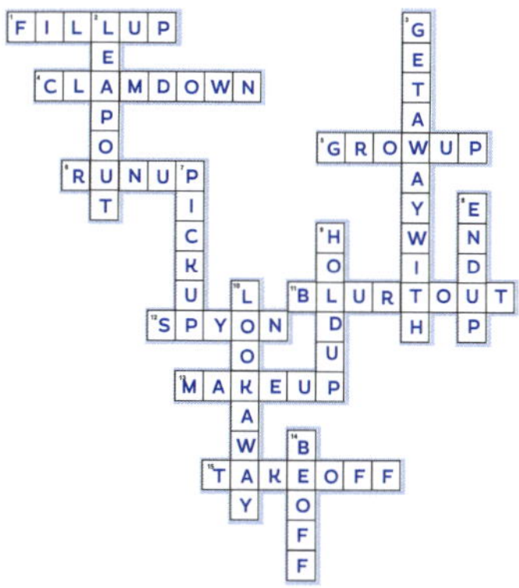

4. LOST IN TRANSLATION?

1 • Tim ran up to Tom and said, "I spied on them all day, they ended up cuddling on the coach."
2 • Tom felt he was paranoid thinking their parents were having a marital breakdown.
3 • She lives in a studio apartment and has a purebred German shepherd, I live in a villa with a basement and a garden and I only have some mangy cats.
4 • He just popped by and said hello, he didn't even take off his jacket. I almost didn't

recognize him, he has grown up so much, he was chubby and chatty!

5 • My teacher always gives me that stern look, her wrinkles scare me, I just have to try to look away and calm down when it happens.

6 • "He won't get away with it! He broke her antique vase and blamed me for it, I don't know why he's so envious, he even tried to report me once!" "Stop whining and stop shouting, this place is crowded, everybody can hear you. He's just a stubborn old man, don't get mad." "You always have to downplay things, I don't like that, I'm off, bye!"

5. LOST IN TRANSLATION?

1 • It was a five-day trip, what a pity it was so short, we got back earlier than we wished.

2 • Let's get to the point Eve, you don't like your job but it takes only ten minutes to get there so you find it convenient, that's why you don't want to quit.

3 • Don't make sailor's promises, stop poking fun at people and find a nice girl to marry!

4 • We arrived late, it took a very long time to get to my future parents-in-law, we just had time to break the ice and then we had to leave again.

5 • "Why doesn't Luis study English?" "I have no clue, maybe because he doesn't like his teacher."

6 • Who cares if they didn't get married? They had a child, all's well that ends well!

6. MAKE IT INDIRECT

1 • "I can play the guitar" Betty said she could play the guitar.

2 • "We will stay in New York" They told us they would stay in New York.

3 • "They arrived a month ago" They told us they had arrived a month ago.

4 • "I have never driven on the right" He admitted he had never driven on the right.

5 • "I can't go to work" He said he couldn't go to work.

6 • "Why don't you like the show?" She wondered why you didn't like the show.

7 • "Where did you go?" He asked where you had gone.

8 • "I'm just having a drink" Susan said she was just having a drink.

7. LOST IN TRANSLATION? MIX IT UP!

"Don't make me regret telling you my secrets."
"Don't worry, I'm not a chatty person." Jane said he could trust her. She picked up her stuff and left. She wondered what kind of secrets he had confessed after all, he just told her he had had an affair with his secretary, but he isn't even married! His secretary is, but it's a minor detail, isn't it? Anyway, "Who cares?", she thought, "I just need to go back home and have a nap".
She got back home, took off her coat and put it in her wonderful walk-in closet, all her friends were so envious of her big house, so big and so neat.

The doorbell rang, it was Jack again, she opened the front door and he blurted out: "Please, keep your mouth shut!" It seemed a bit out of place, she replied that she had got it, there was no need to become paranoid. She said goodbye and went straight to bed. "If he's so worried about getting caught, he shouldn't spit his thoughts out loud as he usually does!" she thought, then fell asleep.

5. MY FAIRY TALE

1. GOT IT?

1 • A mother is telling her daughter the story.
2 • He's an engineer.
3 • They had their first chat in the elevator. They talked about food and what to prepare for a quick but healthy dinner.
4 • He left a bag on her car with some food for her and her dog. She loved it, she smiled and laughed when she saw the bag and the note he wrote.
5 • Her favorite chapter is when one of the protagonists of the book, Bartleboom, talks about the love of his love, his ideal love.
6 • They watched a show in Russian, they didn't understand much but they had fun anyway.
7 • He gave her a white envelope with a piece of paper that was a page he had ripped out of a book. The book was Ocean Sea.
8 • Mr Bartleboom, a thirty-eight-year old man, has been writing love letters for years and he puts them all in a box. He hopes he'll find the right woman for him some day and he imagines that she will find and open the box and read all his letters, or maybe not, but in any case she will smile at him and love him forever.
9 • She's telling her daughter the story because she's only sixteen but she has just had her heart broken for the first time.
10 • She leaves a bottle of water half full on her husband's bedside table with a note, just as he did for her in the past. It was a nice gesture to remember the good old times they had.

2. KEY WORDS

Unable to relax = restless; stomach = gut; friendly = outgoing; to make friends = (to) befriend; a shy person = introverted; a quick look = glance; intentionally = on purpose; common, normal = ordinary; not typical, unusual, original = unique; a person that likes someone and tries to gain their love = wooer; strongly = tightly; impressed strongly = struck (to strike); to look at something/someone deeply = (to) stare at; strong, hard, stubborn = tough; to become curious and interested in something/someone = (to be) intrigued; to express approval by making a quick movement of the head = (to) nod; the center of the city = downtown; shopping center = mall; very big, large in size = huge; not tight, comfortable = loose; a set of clothes worn together = outfit; unexpectedly = by accident; very surprised = astonished; removed, pulled apart = torn; unintentionally, accidentally = by chance

3. FIND THEM OUT!

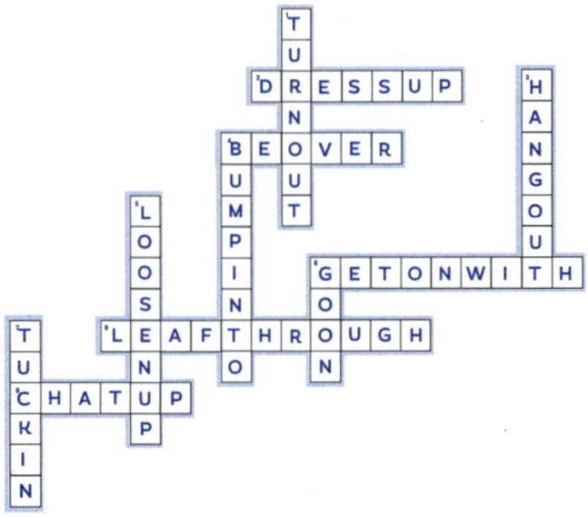

4. LOST IN TRANSLATION?

1. Be careful, he doesn't want to befriend you, he's chatting you up my dear!
2. The teacher went on staring at me, then he said my name and asked me to correct the homework.
3. I went to the mall and bumped into uncle Tony, he said he'll come visit us soon.
4. We used to hang out so much, we had such a good relationship, I can't believe it's over.
5. There's only one thing I'm sure of, you're not an ordinary person! You always dress up to go to work and you're a plumber, you get dirty all the time!

5. LOST IN TRANSLATION?

1 • You'll be thinking I'm a weirdo, but I feel warm fuzzies whenever I see my dog! I'm so in love with him, he's my best friend.

2 • "I followed my gut and I found my Mr Right." "Good for you! What is he like?" "He's so sweet and polite." "And what does he look like?" "He's handsome, very tall, dark hair, blue eyes!"

3 • This time tomorrow I'll be waiting for you at the airport, sweetie.

4 • Whatever you bought me I can't ask for more, I already have everything I need. How about you? Are you happy with what you have?

5 • "I'd like to major in something, now I'm just a jack of all trades and I can't find a job." "You're on the right track, don't worry, the best is yet to come."

6. LOST IN TRANSLATION? MIX IT UP!

Rob: "How are you doing?"
Me: "I'm ok, how about you?"
Rob: "I'm pooped, I've been working all day."
Me: "It's about time! You went to Australia on holiday last month, you're so lucky."
Rob: "I know, I feel so relaxed whenever I think of it. But in the last few days I've

been feeling so restless. I want to change my job."
Me: "What?" Rob: "You must think I'm crazy, but I'm not. Do you remember Kris?"
Me: "Yes, I do!" Rob: "Well, I bumped into her yesterday at the mall and..."
Me: "What does she look like now?"
Rob: "She's gotten old, but she's still nice. She said she was tired of waiting for her dream job so she created it!"
Me: "What does she do?" Rob: "She tells the future by leafing through books. Whatever she finds in the book is really connected to your life somehow, I tried!"
Me: "Really? She's still a weirdo then. She must have followed her gut, I remember she used to do that in high school!"
Rob: "I have a childhood dream too... I want to become a gardener, grow herbs and sell them." Me: "Listen Rob, I know you're tired but let's hang out tonight! Please go back home, dress up and let's go to that fancy new restaurant downtown. I promise that good food will make you feel better!"
Rob was staring at me and I was getting worried but then he patted me on the shoulder and we started to laugh out loud.

6. A DAY AT THE SEASIDE

1. GOT IT?

1 • Six years ago.
2 • The cigarette smoke and hearing them talking.
3 • A pedalo.
4 • Because it is so hot.
5 • The car is parked up the hill and he will have to carry all the equipment.
6 • He's not from England!! He's from Wales! Like Scotland and Northern Ireland, Wales and England are separate states that compose the United Kingdom.
7 • Listening to the rain on the caravan roof.
8 • A car park.
9 • Armbands
10 • Because she was in the toilet.

2. IN OTHER WORDS

He never used to be like that = He wasn't like that in the past;
his wife wasn't that keen on going in the sea = his wife didn't really want to go in the sea;
the sea is packed with people = The sea is full of people;
doesn't seem to be of the same opinion = doesn't seem to agree;
he's not the bravest of swimmers = he's not the most courageous of swimmers

3. KEY WORDS

Gorgeous = beautiful; to matter = to be important; to shiver = to shake due to being cold; to queue = stand in a line to wait for something (like in a supermarket);

to be worth it = useful and rewarding, despite the difficulty; purse = a small container for money (like a wallet) typically for women; to dig = to break up/ remove earth with a machine or tool; edge = the outside limit of an area or object; shore = the land along the edge of the sea; shins = the front part of the leg below the knee; fierce = aggressive; eager = enthusiastic; to be mistaken = to be wrong; rudely = impolitely; belongings = the things you own; bearable = can be endured

4. FIND THEM OUT!

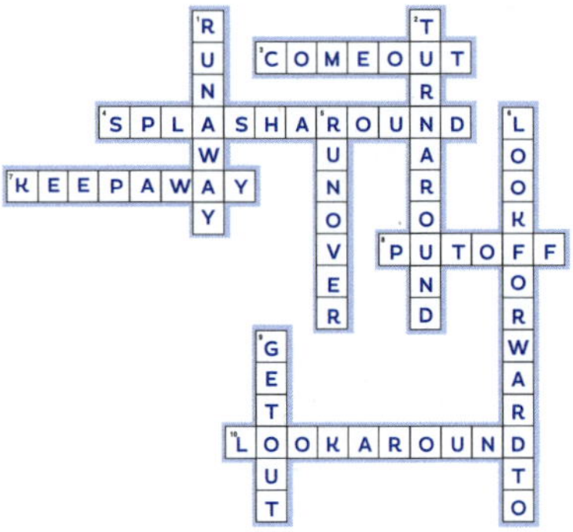

5. EXERCISE - IDIOMS/SLANG & MORE

1 • OK, he has an amazing body and a handsome face and all that, but his arrogant attitude just puts me off.

2 • I don't like to put too much money on my pre-paid credit card, I think it's better to be safe than sorry.

3 • "Would you like any more chips with your fish?" "No, that will do, thanks."

4 • You should have seen the look on my wife's face when she saw me in the supermarket with another woman, if looks could kill...

5 • The dog next door never stops barking, it's really starting to get on my nerves.

6 • His parents have always preferred his brother, but now that he doesn't live with them anymore it doesn't bother him.

7 • "I want to go to the bank before we leave town, is that OK?" "Yeah, I don't mind."

6. EXTRA VOCAB

Petto: Chest; Mento: Chin; Fronte: Forehead; Guancia: Cheek; Vita: Waist; Coscia: Thigh; Stinco: Shin; Dita delle mani: Fingers; Dita dei piedi: Toes; Spalla: Shoulder; Collo: Neck; Polso: Wrist; Gomito: Elbow; Tallone: Heel; Caviglia: Ankle; Polpaccio: Calf.

7. LOST IN TRANSLATION?

1 • "Why wasn't Elena at the party?" "I don't know, she must have decided not to go."
2 • When I was a child it was a problem for me to eat vegetables, but now I'm used to them.
3 • I can't ask her to live with me, we hardly know each other.
4 • If you had asked me, I would have gone to the shop with you.
5 • No matter how much I try, I don't think I'll ever get used to the Scottish accent.
6 • That physics exam was so difficult, it was hardly worth studying for it.
7 • I see you bought the latest ZPhone, you should have got the Trident, it is cheaper and much better.
8 • I could have helped my wife do the washing up, but I was so tired.
9 • This chicken is hardly cooked.
10 • I've always worked part time, I'm not used to working long hours.

8. LOST IN TRANSLATION? MIX IT UP!

Adrian didn't mind not having a girlfriend, he was used to it because he had hardly had any women in his life since he was a teenager. However, he was a funny guy, and so women loved spending time with him, he used to make them laugh their heads off with his jokes. One day, he was driving his car when he was distracted by a man with a big chin, he turned around to look at it, he wasn't watching where he was going and ran over a woman who was crossing the road. He quickly got out of the car to see if she was ok, he saw the look on her face, if looks could kill... It was then that he noticed that she was gorgeous, she had a really beautiful forehead and Adrian was eager to make sure she was ok. He asked if she was ok, and she said that her thigh was hurting but that it doesn't matter because she's got another leg. Adrian laughed. He was quickly falling in love with her, he wanted to ask her out on a date, but he was worried that she wouldn't be keen on him, but he decided to be brave and ask anyway, and he could hardly believe it when she said yes! And now, ten years later, they are married with two children, and he knows that if he hadn't run that woman over that day, he would never have met the girl of his dreams.

7. LUC & SARAH

1. GOT IT?

1 • She picked up (grabbed) her bag.
2 • That the whole world was still asleep.
3 • That something would happen to show she had made the right decisions in life.
4 • Because the traffic jams were going in the opposite direction.
5 • Because he had nothing in particular planned for the day, just routine work.
6 • Because the bunch of flowers was so big.

7 • That the woman's voice sounded so masculine.
8 • The group of girls.
9 • Because her dinner arrived.
10 • To keep other women away from him.

2. IN OTHER WORDS

in no more than twenty minutes = in less than twenty minutes; he was supposed to go last night = he should have gone last night; Patricia was always very sunny and helpful = Patricia was always very cheerful/happy and helpful; Helen could hardly breathe = Helen was having great difficulty breathing; and started a long rehearsed speech = and started a speech he had practiced many times

3. KEY WORDS

Autopilot = doing something without thinking about it; kettle = a container for boiling water; make-up = cosmetic products for enhancing the appearance; to grab (sth) = to take something quickly; commuter = a person who travels a significant distance to get to work; to oversleep = to sleep longer than intended; boot = a space in a car for carrying items; flexi-time = a system that enables employees to work flexible hours; firmly = in a strong way; to water = when the eyes start to fill with water; to be blocked up = when breathing through the nose is difficult due a cold or allergy; awkward = difficult or embarrassing; slim = thin; to spot = to see or notice someone/something; gaze = a long look; strikingly = in a way that attracts attention

4. FIND THEM OUT!

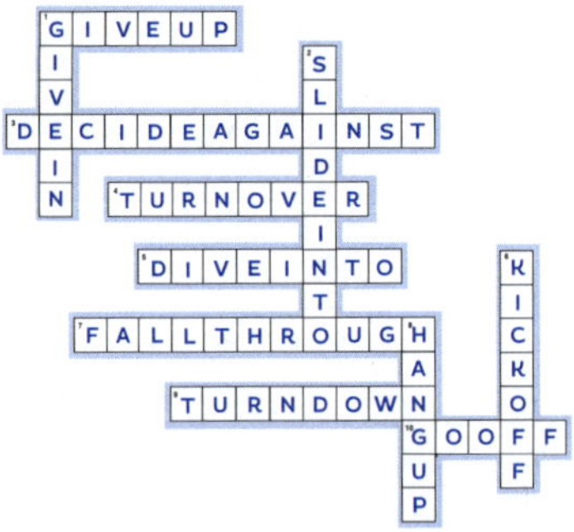

5. EXERCISE - IDIOMS/SLANG & MORE

1 • You are older than your sister, you should be setting her an example.
2 • He's never had trouble getting women, he just has something about him that they seem to like.
3 • My brother has a reputation for being mean, indeed, he's always the last one to buy a round in the pub.
4 • Please, just get straight to the point, are you going to sack me or not?
5 • They introduced themselves and exchanged pleasantries before starting the negotiation.

6 • I had put up with his complaining for years, but when he told me I was starting to look fat, I had to leave him, it was the straw that broke the camel's back.

6. BE PASSIVE

Every single movement was done on auto-pilot;
all the windows had been opened;
and the flowers had been distributed;
the decision to join him was made in about 3.5 seconds;
the gym was postponed, once again;
was invited in;
Luc's attention was immediately drawn to a group of girls;
the conversation was cut short by Sarah's phone ringing;

7. LOST IN TRANSLATION?

1 • Last week John Lennon's guitar was sold at auction, it was bought by an anonymous collector.
2 • When you contact the sales department you need to speak to either Mr Taylor or Ms Walker.
3 • I have already lost five kilos, but to reach my target I need to lose another eleven.
4 • Paul was supposed to send the end-of-month report to the CEO today, but he's already gone home, he must have forgotten.
5 • Will the car be repaired before Ms Dean returns?
6 • We need to find another £10,000, if not, we won't be able to buy our dream house.
7 • When you become resident in a foreign country you are supposed to pay tax in that country.
8 • Has the letter been written yet? It was supposed to be sent yesterday.

8. LOST IN TRANSLATION? MIX IT UP!

It was supposed to be the perfect job, she had even turned down a job offer from Syntax, Inc. and decided against another two attractive job offers. However, a recent awkward feedback meeting with Ms Miller, during which she had been firmly criticised, was the straw that broke the camel's back. When she started this new job she dived straight into it, trying to set an example to her new team, but now she was ready to give up and throw all her things into the boot of her car and go home. The journey home would take no more than forty minutes, where she would be able to switch the kettle on, grab a packet of biscuits, slide into her dressing gown and watch her favourite films all night before oversleeping the next morning... But then the dream ended, she was supposed to attend another meeting in 10 minutes, this time with Steve. Steve was slim and had something about him, she didn't want to miss it, maybe this time she would finally get straight to the point and ask him out to dinner... maybe!

8. CHRISTMAS

1. GOT IT?

1 • Because she has moved around so much she doesn't really know where she is from.
2 • When the children open their presents.
3 • Because there are ornaments everywhere that she is worried could get broken.
4 • Because there is too much furniture and so there is no space for a bed.
5 • The shortcuts.
6 • Because Emma's mother-in-law has a rule that everyone must be together.
7 • Because the clock stopped working. He had another beer.
8 • Because he things they should be cooked for a very short period of time.

2. IN OTHER WORDS

Christmas journeys are always particularly eventful = Christmas journeys are always very interesting;
A bit of snow fell on London = A little snow fell on London;
They gave each other a puzzled look = They gave each other a confused look;
Mark was in charge of peas = Mark was responsible for peas;
try to calm him down = try to make him less angry;

3. KEY WORDS

Eve = the day or period before an important event; eventful = full of interesting things or events; back and forth = constantly moving or travelling between two places; chest of drawers = an item of furniture that consists of a series of drawers; dressing table = an item of furniture that consists of a table, mirror and drawers, normally used for getting dressed or applying make up; carpet = a floor covering made of fabric; chip = a small piece broken from a hard material; airbed = an inflatable mattress; armchair = a single, large, comfortable chair with supports for the arms; bottom = the part of the body you sit on (buttocks); numb = without feeling; to simmer = to boil gently; to peel = to remove the outer skin of a vegetable (e.g. a potato); shortcut = a shorter or quicker way of doing something; sleigh = a vehicle or platform pulled by animals; turnip = a root vegetable, normally white and round; touchy = very sensitive and easily offended; unmentionable = cannot be spoken about

4. EXERCISE - IDIOMS/SLANG & MORE

1 • I hate it when someone talks about me behind my back.
2 • You select tools, options, general settings then click "show profile pictures" and Bob's your uncle, your picture will appear the next time you log in.
3 • When Steve makes fun of people he thinks he's being funny, but he's not, people find it irritating.
4 • Oh, by the way, your husband called, he said it's nothing to worry about, he'll

call back later.

5 • Damn, I lost track of time, the meeting started 10 minutes ago and I'm supposed to be there.

6 • I'm having nothing to do with this project, you just want everything done your way.

7 • The interview went quite well. They said that they'll call me by the end of the week to let me know, fingers crossed.

5. LOST IN TRANSLATION?

1 • My second cousin is very disappointed with her house, she thinks her husband's mother should buy them a bigger one.

2 • If he had gone to bed earlier, he might not have woken up so late.

3 • I'm so excited about our holiday, I hope that my great grandmother doesn't get bored.

4 • Our fish are scared of the woman next door's cat, but when I speak to her about it she says it doesn't matter.

5 • My great aunt's garden is great, I find the vegetable garden particularly interesting.

6 • "Jason, I'm leaving you, I've been having an affair with your sister's husband and we're in love." "It doesn't matter to me, now I can finally go and live abroad."

7 • Dennis's dad gave him that name because it was his great grandfather's friend's name.

8 • That goal they scored last night was surprising, but I was more amazed by the cheerleaders.

9 • If it doesn't stop raining, we can't go to the beach.

10 • We would have more money if we didn't work for the Government.

6. LOST IN TRANSLATION? MIX IT UP!

New year's eve is always eventful for my father, stepmother and half-sister. I don't have anything to do with their new year's eve parties anymore, in the past I just sat on my bottom in the armchair and got bored. Last year they invited the whole family, grandparents, great grandparents, cousins, second cousins, I think I was the only one who wasn't interested in attending. Anyway, I don't like to talk about people behind their backs, especially my own family, but apparently they all lost track of time and spent the whole night drinking. You should have seen my father's wife's face in the morning when she saw the mess. There were people sleeping everywhere, on airbeds, on the carpet, one person on the dressing table, there was even someone sleeping on the sleigh in the garden. When she saw that all her ornaments and precious plates had been chipped, she was shocked. After spending thirty minutes running back and forth trying to clean everything up, she decided that it was pointless being disappointed, "it doesn't matter" she said.

9. SATURDAY NIGHT

1. GOT IT?

1 • Because his girlfriend was away at her parents' house.
2 • Because the pub was busy, there was nowhere to sit down.
3 • He's getting old, so he's not able to drink like he used to.
4 • Because she hated the fact that he couldn't dance.
5 • Because his injuries were so bad.
6 • He was worried that perhaps the police believed he had hurt Miles, and he was worried that it might be true.
7 • He hears someone make a noise by clearing their throat.
8 • Because it means nothing serious happened.

2. IN OTHER WORDS

appointment set for around 8 pm = appointment made/fixed for about 8 pm;
wow, that sounds awful = wow, that sounds terrible;
I'm a bit nervous about what it can do = I'm a bit worried about what it can do;
he escorts me into an office = he takes/accompanies me to an office;
but now keeping our drinks close by = but now keeping our drinks nearby;

3. KEY WORDS

real ale = traditional British beer, unpasteurized and unfiltered; rush hour = the period of the day when road traffic is at its heaviest; takeaway = a meal bought from a shop or restaurant and eaten elsewhere; to crawl = to move using the hands and knees; drunkenness = the state of being drunk; scar = the mark left on the skin after a cut or injury has healed; row = argument; dizzy = the sensation of spinning and feeling that you could fall; to struggle = to have difficulty doing something; to faint = to suddenly and momentarily become unconscious; to turn pale = to lose colour in the face; inadvertently = unintentionally; giggle = a little laugh; stained = to have a mark on it or be discoloured; to spike = to add alcohol or a drug to someone's drink/food; to harm = to injure or hurt someone; prank = a practical joke; speechless = to be unable to say anything, normally through shock or surprise; odd = strange, unusual; to fancy = to want something

4. FIND THEM OUT!

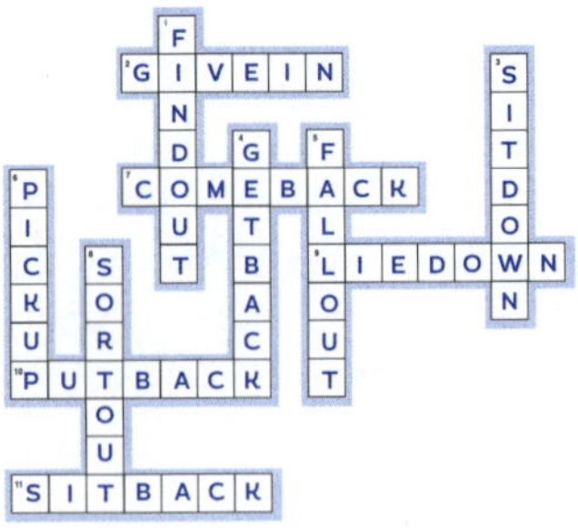

5. EXERCISE - IDIOMS/SLANG & MORE

1 • My heart sank when the doctor told me I had diabetes.
2 • When the lottery company phoned to tell us we had won the lottery, I just couldn't believe my ears.
3 • My girlfriend is always trying to convince me that we should tie the knot but I'm happy with our relationship the way it is.
4 • I'm lost for words, someone has scratched the side of our brand new car.
5 • "Please don't cut my hair Mum. If you do they'll take the mickey out of me at school."
6 • I dread to think what my dad will do to me when he finds out I've broken his fishing rod.
7 • I'm just pulling your leg, I didn't really play professional football for Barcelona when I was young.

6. LOST IN TRANSLATION?

1 • Australia is such a lovely place, I've already been there four times and I'm going back next year.
2 • I've got a sore throat, a toothache and a pain in my hip, today is such a terrible day.
3 • We always have fun when we spend the evening with Steve and Angela.
4 • Chris worked as an accountant in 1999, now he sells carpets.
5 • They've got such good children, especially the youngest one.
6 • I've had this headache for over a week, I think it's time I made an appointment to see the doctor.
7 • I'm thinking of going to Greece on holiday, my brother has been there and he said it's beautiful.
8 • I've got such a sore wrist, it hurts whenever I try to type on the PC.

7. LOST IN TRANSLATION? MIX IT UP!

They have been neighbours since they were children, and during that time they have always been such good friends, but something just happened. The situation is actually quite funny, it all started while Valentina was lying down enjoying a drink when suddenly she started to feel a bit dizzy and she heard a loud noise. She struggled to stand up due to her backache and sore knee, but she eventually crawled outside and saw that a large piece of plastic had hit her car, that's odd, she thought, then her heart sank. She looked up and couldn't believe her eyes, a piece of plastic had broken away from a cupboard on her neighbour's balcony, at that point her neighbour came out and the row started. During the row Valentina turned pale with anger until eventually her neighbour gave in, accepted it was her fault and promised to sort out the damage to the car. They then sat down together and giggled about the argument they had just had. "That was such a stupid row, do you fancy having a drink with me?" Valentina said.

10. A NEW CAR

1. Ae vs Be

1• Let's go to the shopping centre, put the shopping bags in the boot of the car.
2• The train will arrive soon, our holiday is about to start.
3• When you stop the car in the petrol station you should always put the handbrake on.
4• I told the cashier in the shop that I didn't want to buy the packet of biscuits.
5• It's normally a good idea to put your pants on before you put your trousers on, if you do it the other way round people might laugh at you.
6• I drove on the motorway in a grey car that didn't have a bonnet, when the police stopped me they asked me for my driving licence.
7• When you get to the car park, can you put the rubbish in the rubbish bin please?
8• I've been playing football ever since I got out of the pushchair.

2. KEY WORDS

second-hand = not new, has had a previous owner
classified ad = a small and short advertisement in a magazine or newspaper
nickname = a familiar name that substitutes a person's real name
to mishear = to fail to hear something correctly
livid = very angry
bridesmaid = a person (female) who assists and accompanies a bride at their wedding
fence = a structure (made of wood, for example) that encloses an area (e.g. garden)
slightly = to a small degree
to slam = to shut something (e.g. a door) very firmly
rude = impolite or insulting
crystal ball = a glass ball used by fortune teller to see into the future
weird = strange
convertible = a car that can be converted by removing the roof
to pack = to put some things in a bag, suitcase or other type of container
helmet = protective equipment for the head
fan = a person who follows and supports a person (e.g. pop star) or team (e.g. sports team)

3. EXERCISE - IDIOMS/SLANG & MORE

1 • Don't feel sorry for me, it's my fault that I lost my job.
2 • I'm always the one cracking jokes at dinner parties, but some people don't find me funny.
3 • I can't talk right now, I'm in a rush, can I call you back tomorrow?
4 • I've just bought a brand new car and I've scratched it already, I should have followed my son-in-law's advice and bought a second-hand one.

5 • Get out of my office at once, if you are still here when I count to ten, I'll sack you.
6 • Once the book was published it sold 10,000 copies in no time at all.
7 • It was a bad line so I didn't catch what he said about next week's meeting.
8 •. If you had remembered to bring the satnav, we would have arrived on time.

4. LOST IN TRANSLATION?

1 • We've got a lot of eggs in the fridge.
2 • I have always wanted to run my own company, but you need a lot of money for the initial investment and I haven't got much.
3 • I spent years driving my dad's car, when I bought my own one I was so proud of it I drove it up and down our street for days.
4 • UK speaker: "Wow! You've got the new Tarantino DVD. Can I borrow it please?"
US speaker: "No, I didn't watch it yet."
5 • Edward made this cake on his own, he's only 9 years old, a lot of children of the same age couldn't do that.
6 • "How much water are you supposed to drink every day?" "I'm not sure, but it's a lot."
7 • If you go down the path, through the gate, turn left and then walk up the road, you'll find the supermarket after about 300 metres.
8 • "How long have you owned a yacht?" "Actually, I don't have my own yacht, I just own an agency that sells them."

5. LOST IN TRANSLATION? MIX IT UP!

She had never owned her own violin because she didn't have much money and could never afford a brand new one. One day, as she was walking down the street she saw a second-hand violin in a shop window, she fell in love with it at once and despite the fact that it cost a lot of money, she knew she had to own it. She was in a rush as she was going on holiday and she still hadn't packed her bags. She ran down the road, jumped over a fence and pushed past some shoppers, she knew it was rude but she didn't feel sorry for them, all she cared about was that violin. She jumped into her convertible car, slammed the door, put her helmet on (she cared a lot about safety) and drove down the road, she had to get home to get the money for the violin. She put the satnav on and got home in no time at all, but when she got inside the house, she couldn't believe her eyes, her house had been burgled. Her money, her passport, her purse, all gone. She wanted to crack a joke to make herself feel better, but she knew it would be weird, so she just sat there, felt sorry for herself and cried... no jokes, no holiday, no violin.

NOTE

NOTE 

INDICE

AMERICAN ENGLISH

The American Dream - Story 1........................p. 8
Exercises - Story 1 ....p. 13
What a Holiday! - Story 2 ....p. 21
Exercises - Story 2...............................p. 26
A Sleepless Night - Story 3 ....p. 35
Exercises - Story 3............................... p. 41
A Dog's Life - Story 4..............................p. 51
Exercises - Story 4 ....p. 58
My Fairy Tale - Story 5.............................p. 70
Exercises - Story 5...............................p. 76

BRITISH ENGLISH

A Day at the Seaside - Story 6......................p. 86
Exercises - Story 6...............................p. 92
Luc & Sarah - Story 7 ....p. 102
Exercises - Story 7 .... p. 108
Christmas - Story 8................................. p. 117
Exercises - Story 8...............................p. 124
Saturday Night - Story 9 ....p. 134
Exercises - Story 9...............................p. 140
The New Car - Story 10 .... p. 151
Exercises - Story 10..............................p. 158

SOLUTIONS ....p. 166